A DISCOURSE ON IN

JEAN-JACQUES ROUSSEAU was born in Geneva in 1712. Abandoned by his father at the age of ten he tried his hand as an engraver's apprentice before he left the city in 1728. From then on he was to wander Europe seeking an elusive happiness. At Turin he became a Catholic convert, and as a footman, seminarist, music teacher or tutor visited many parts of Switzerland and France. In 1732 he settled for eight years at Chambéry or at Les Charmettes, the country house of Madame de Warens, remembered by Rousseau as an idyllic place in the *Confessions*. In 1741 he set out for Paris, where he met Diderot, who commissioned him to write the music articles for the *Encyclopédie*. In the meantime he fathered five children by Thérèse Levasseur, a servant girl, and abandoned them to a foundling home. The 1750s witnessed a breach with Voltaire and Diderot, and his writing struck a new note of defiant independence. In his *Discours sur les sciences et les arts* and the *Discours sur l'origine de l'inégalité* he showed how the growth of civilization corrupted natural goodness and increased inequality between men. In 1758 he attacked his former friends, the Encyclopaedists, in the *Lettre à d'Alembert sur les spectacles* which pilloried cultured society. In 1757 he moved to Montmorency and these five years were the most fruitful of his life. His remarkable novel *La Nouvelle Héloise* (1761) met with immediate and enormous success. In this and in *Émile*, which followed a year later, Rousseau invoked the inviolability of personal ideals against the powers of the state and the pressures of society. The crowning achievement of his political philosophy was *The Social Contract*, published in 1762. That same year he wrote an attack on revealed religion, the *Profession de foi du vicaire savoyard*. He was driven from Switzerland and fled to England, where he succeeded only in making an enemy of Hume and returned to his continental peregrinations. In 1770 Rousseau completed his *Confessions*. His last years were spent largely in France, where he died in 1778.

MAURICE CRANSTON was born in London in 1920 and was educated at London University and St Catherine's College, Oxford. For twenty-six years he was Professor of Political Science at the London School of

Economics. He also held a number of visiting professorships and was a former President of the Institut International de Philosophie Politique. His 1957 biography of John Locke remains the definitive study of Locke's life. His many other books include *Human Rights Today*, *The Mask of Politics* and *Philosophers and Pamphleteers: Political Theorists of the French Enlightenment*, as well as two translations of Rousseau's works, *The Social Contract* and *A Discourse on Inequality*, both published in Penguin Classics. More recently his two volumes of biography on Rousseau, *Jean-Jacques: the Early Life and Work of Jean-Jacques Rousseau 1712–1754* and *The Noble Savage* appeared to great critical acclaim. He was working on a third volume at the time of his death in 1993.

Jean-Jacques Rousseau

A DISCOURSE ON INEQUALITY

TRANSLATED
WITH AN INTRODUCTION
AND NOTES BY

MAURICE CRANSTON

PENGUIN BOOKS

PENGUIN BOOKS

Published by the Penguin Group
Penguin Books Ltd, 80 Strand, London WC2R 0RL, England
Penguin Putnam Inc., 375 Hudson Street, New York, New York 10014, USA
Penguin Books Australia Ltd, 250 Camberwell Road, Camberwell, Victoria 3124, Australia
Penguin Books Canada Ltd, 10 Alcorn Avenue, Toronto, Ontario, Canada M4V 3B2
Penguin Books India (P) Ltd, 11 Community Centre, Panchsheel Park, New Delhi – 110 017, India
Penguin Books (NZ) Ltd, Cnr Rosedale and Airborne Roads, Albany, Auckland, New Zealand
Penguin Books (South Africa) (Pty) Ltd, 24 Sturdee Avenue, Rosebank 2196, South Africa

Penguin Books Ltd, Registered Offices: 80 Strand, London WC2R 0RL, England

www.penguin.com

This translation first published 1984

045

Copyright © Maurice Cranston, 1984
All rights reserved

Printed in England by Clays Ltd, St Ives plc
Filmset in Monophoto Bembo

Except in the United States of America, this book is sold subject
to the condition that it shall not, by way of trade or otherwise, be lent,
re-sold, hired out, or otherwise circulated without the publisher's
prior consent in any form of binding or cover other than that in
which it is published and without a similar condition including this
condition being imposed on the subsequent purchaser

ISBN-13: 978-0-140-44439-1

www.greenpenguin.co.uk

Penguin Books is committed to a sustainable
future for our business, our readers and our planet.
This book is made from Forest Stewardship
Council™ certified paper.

CONTENTS

Foreword	7
Introduction	9
Discourse on the Origins and Foundations of Inequality among Men	55
Rousseau's Notes	139
Abbreviations used in Editor's Introduction and Notes	173
Editor's Notes	175

FOREWORD

This translation is based on the text published by Marc-Michel Rey in 1755. Additional material which appeared in the Moulton-Du Peyrou edition of 1782 is printed in footnotes marked by an asterisk. The original MS. used by Rey has been lost, as has the manuscript submitted by Rousseau to the Academy of Dijon; only a few fragments of an earlier draft of the *Discourse* survive.*

---

* See R. A. Leigh, 'Manuscrits disparus de J.-J. Rousseau', *Annales*, XXXIV (1956–8).

INTRODUCTION

ROUSSEAU'S *Discourse on the Origins of Inequality* is dedicated to the sovereign citizens of Geneva, and pays homage to that republic in language which some readers have considered suspiciously fulsome. Rousseau describes his native city-state as a republic ideal in size, a place where no man is above the law, where age and experience have mellowed the constitution and where the right to legislate belongs to all the citizens:

> The more I reflect on your civil and political arrangements the less can I imagine that the nature of human contrivance could produce anything better ... Your happiness is already achieved, you have only to know how to be satisfied with it ... You have no masters other than wise laws made by yourselves and administered by upright magistrates of your own choosing.[1]

These words may well sound strange to anyone familiar with Rousseau's *Letters from the Mountains*[2] in which he describes the regime in Geneva as an odious and lawless despotism, but it must be remembered that Rousseau wrote these *Letters* when he was aged fifty-two, in 1764, after he and his books had been outlawed by the authorities of Geneva, and after he had been amply briefed on the politics of Geneva by opponents, both moderate and radical, of the regime. Up to the age of forty-two, when he wrote his *Discourse on Inequality*, he was an uncritical patriot.

Geneva in 1712, when Rousseau was born there, was a singular political entity. With an entire population of little more than 25,000, it had been an independent nation for more than a century and a half, one of the few surviving city-states in an age of great kingdoms and royal absolutism. Although it was not an ancient republic like Venice or San Marino, or even a Free City within the Holy Roman Empire, the burghers of Geneva had already in the Middle Ages exploited the rivalry between their two feudal masters, the Bishops and secular lords of Geneva to secure themselves a large measure of civil autonomy. At the beginning of the fifteenth century when their secular lords, the Earls of Savoy, became Dukes and made strenuous efforts to assert their sovereignty in Geneva at the expense of the

1. *OC*, III, pp. 115–16.   2. *OC*, III, pp. 683–897.

Bishop, the Bishop made correspondingly generous offers to the burghers to win their support against the Duke. They backed him in return for a contract which recognized their General Council – the public assembly to which every citizen belonged – as the central legislative body of the city.[3] Thus, Geneva, while still a municipality, acquired the structures and some of the political experience on which an independent republic could be built.

But independence did not come until another century. The Dukes of Savoy, ambitious and successful monarchs, destined in time to assume the full majesty of Kings, continued to assert their claims to Geneva, even though its value as a prize diminished somewhat when it lost to Lyons its pre-eminence as a centre of international trade fairs and its prosperity and population declined in turn. The Dukes used cunning as well as force to uphold their sovereignty; from 1449 until 1522 they had a number of their own family enthroned as Bishop of Geneva to thwart the burghers' manoeuvres to pit one palace against another. Besides, not all Genevans objected to active Savoyard rule, which seemed to some to offer the only hope for economic renewal. Duke Philibert, who entered Geneva in person in 1501, introduced merriment and gaiety as well as more prosperity into the life of the city, and earned some genuine popularity.[4] There emerged among the burghers a faction known as 'Marmalukes', who supported the Savoyard connection; their opponents were called 'Eidgenots' because they favoured instead federation (*Eidgenossen*) with the neighbouring cantons of Switzerland. Neither party at that time – the earlier years of the sixteenth century – proposed what was soon to come about, the institution of Geneva as a fully autonomous republic.

Such an outcome was indeed unlikely to have been desired. For how could Geneva be expected to defend itself? It was not situated like San Marino on the top of a mountain, or surrounded like Venice by water; it was located at the foot of the Alps, accessible by all the roads that had once led to its fairs. If Geneva was no longer to be defended as part of the Duchy of Savoy, the sensible alternative was seen as developing from *combourgeoisie* with the neighbouring cantons of Berne and Fribourg into full membership of the Swiss

3. P. Bertrand, *Survol de l'histoire de Genève*, p. 44.
4. I. Spon, *History of Geneva*, p. 43.

INTRODUCTION

Confederation. The Reformation thwarted this design; for Berne adopted the Reformed religion and Fribourg remained loyal to Catholicism, so that Geneva could not join one canton in its religious settlement without antagonizing the other. In the event, Berne, stronger in military force and offering more help to Geneva in its resistance to the Savoyards, prevailed over Fribourg.

It was in 1534 that the burghers of Geneva rid themselves at once of their Bishop and their allegiance to Savoy, and, by striking money, proclaimed themselves a state. When the Savoyards threatened invasion a year later, the Bernese offered the Genevans incorporation, like that of the *pays de Vaud*, under their government. The Genevans, having no wish to exchange the domination of Chambéry for the domination of Berne, refused; but since the Bernese troops were desperately needed, they could not decently refuse a rapprochement with Berne in the matter of religion, so they declared themselves Protestant, a move which also served usefully to justify the permanent exclusion of the Catholic Bishop. One result of this was to alienate not only Fribourg but all the other Catholic Swiss cantons, so that Geneva's adhesion to that Confederation was vetoed for generations to come. Geneva became an independent republic because it could not become (and did not become until 1817) a canton in Switzerland.

The Reformed religion did not appeal immediately to everyone in Geneva; there were those who felt closer to Fribourg, with its French-speaking Catholic culture, than to patrician, German-speaking Berne; many to whom the theology of Luther and Zwingli was altogether foreign. Providentially, from the point of view of the Reformed religion, a solution to this problem appeared in the person of Jean Calvin, a French theologian of undoubted genius, a great preacher and a systematic thinker, with a different set of Protestant ideas from those of Luther and Zwingli, and also a prophet in the style of Savonarola, with a similar dream of realizing on earth the dream of a truly Christian commonwealth. Here was a man to turn a political necessity into a spiritual achievement, a revolutionary man for a revolutionary moment, a practical visionary who could transform a medieval bishopric into a modern city-state, and reconcile Genevans to the Reformed religion by changing both, remodelling the doctrine and compelling every single inhabitant to stand up and be converted. Rousseau thought of Calvin as a great Law-giver who had invented the constitution of the republic of Geneva, a founder like Lycurgus or Solon. If modern historians[5] see Calvin rather as one who adapted the traditional municipal institutions to serve the purposes of sovereign independence, Calvin's importance for Rousseau was governed by what he believed to have happened rather than what actually happened. There can be no doubting that Calvin was remarkably successful in presiding over Geneva's formative years as an autonomous state, and he owed his success in part to the lucky circumstances that throughout the years of his residence in Geneva – from 1536 to 1568 – the territories surrounding the city were occupied by Protestant Bernese troops, so that he was able to reorganize Geneva without hostile intervention by the Catholic Savoyards, whose forces at other times stood on the frontiers of the city.

Calvin was fortunate again in that the persecution of Protestants in France brought refugees sympathetic to his purposes into Geneva, which enabled him to enlarge with immigrants a roll of citizens which was diminished by his own harsh policy of expelling from the city all those native Genevans who resisted conversion to the Reformed religion. Geneva became almost as much as was Massachusetts afterwards a commonwealth of exiles united by a puritan ideology. The new men brought new trades, industries and wealth;[6] and Geneva became an industrial, financial and commercial metropolis. Calvin's academies and seminaries attracted scholars from all over Europe, and although one or two such visitors in Calvin's lifetime found that they had only exchanged one form of persecution for another – Michel Servet, for example, being burned at the stake for socinianism, and Jacques Gruet put to death for atheism – religious fanaticism died down as Geneva grew richer.

Calvin no less than Lycurgus and Solon was in Rousseau's mind when he wrote the famous chapter in the *Social Contract* on 'The Law-giver'; and the fundamental laws which Calvin drafted for Geneva were more than anything else the inspiration for the constitution of the republic which Rousseau sketches in that same book: indeed he says as much in his *Letters from the Mountains*, where he tells the

5. See, for example, *Histoire de Genève des origines à 1789*, Geneva, 1951.
6. Louis Binz, *Brève Histoire de Genève*, 1981, pp. 30–37.

Genevans: 'I took your constitution, which I considered good, as my model for political institutions.'[7] There were important differences between the forms of government laid down in the constitution and the ways in which eighteenth-century Geneva was actually run, and although Rousseau was acutely aware of these when he wrote *Letters from the Mountains*, we must remember that at the time he was working on the *Discourse on Inequality* he had not looked far behind the splendidly republican façade.

The main institutions of the Genevan system were the General Council, the Council of Two Hundred and the Council of Twenty-Five, modified forms of the municipal councils of the medieval bishopric. The General Council was composed of all the citizens and burgesses, that is, of every male person over twenty-five years old who had the right to be registered on the rolls. In principle this was the sovereign body of the state, with powers to make laws, to elect the principal magistrates, to approve or reject proposals concerning alliances, the raising of loans, the building of fortifications, the imposition of taxes and the declaration of war. It was required to meet twice a year for the election of magistrates, and otherwise whenever summoned by the Councils of Two Hundred or Twenty-Five. In the General Council there were no debates, and no measure could be initiated. Debates took place in the smaller councils, and the General Council voted mutely on proposals which issued from them. The Council of Two Hundred was designed not only to deliberate on policies to submit to the General Council, but to be the supreme court of justice, to have the power of pardoning, and to elect the Council of Twenty-Five. This Council of Twenty-Five was the executive instrument of the republic. Its members, elected from the ranks of the Council of Two Hundred, were members for life. It was formally responsible for all decisions that did not require the convocation of the Two Hundred; it had the power of judging all criminal causes (without the power of pardon, which the Two Hundred possessed), the hearing of all civil causes, the nomination of public servants, the administration of finances, together with the right to summon the Council of Two Hundred at its discretion

---

7. *OC*, III, p. 1660–61. Otherwise, Rousseau adds, his *Social Contract* would only have been another Utopia like Plato's *Republic* (see C. W. Hendel, *J.-J. Rousseau*, vol. II, p. 295).

and to have all the principal magistrates chosen from its own ranks.

This distribution of duties was conceived by Calvin as providing a felicitous balance between the democratic element represented by the General Council and the aristocratic element represented by the life-tenured members of the Council of Twenty-Five, a balance which he considered advantageous from the point of view of the third, and to Calvin, the most important element in the state, the theocratic, represented by the Church and its institutions, the Consistory, which controlled people's morals by elaborate surveillance, the Company of Pastors and the Academy, which guided culture and opinion.

Between the middle of the sixteenth century, when Calvin reformed the constitution, and the early years of the eighteenth century, when Rousseau was born, a number of important changes took place in the city, and these changes were both political and social. Without any formal constitutional change, the powers of the Council of Twenty-Five became systematically enlarged at the expense of the Council of Two Hundred and even more at the expense of the citizenry assembled in the General Council.[8] The Council of Twenty-Five came wholly to dominate the Council of Two Hundred, and in the end the General Council was summoned only to rubberstamp the decisions of the magistrates.

Social changes added a further dimension to these developments. Among the French and Italian Protestants who found refuge in Geneva were several from noble families who brought with them not only their wealth, but their assumed right to lead and rule. These families monopolized the places on the Council of Twenty-Five, and by excluding all others set up what was in fact the rule of a hereditary nobility – not an open and avowed patriciate like that of Berne, but a patriciate veiled by the ceremonies and styles and language of republicanism. What was not disguised was the social superiority of these patrician families, and Geneva being a city on a hill, they were able to proclaim their superiority by building their elegant houses on the upper levels around the Hôtel de Ville, while the humbler families crowded in wooden dwellings on the damp shores of the river and the lake.

Social change of another kind took place at about the same

8. René Guerdan, *Histoire de Genève*, Paris, 1981, pp. 155–66. See also J. S. Spink, *J.-J. Rousseau et Genève*, Paris, 1934, pp. 1–8.

period. The number of residents of Geneva who qualified as citizens became proportionately smaller as the population grew from about 13,000 in Calvin's time to 25,000 in Rousseau's. In the sixteenth century the great majority of male residents were citizens; by the eighteenth century the citizens constituted a minority. Only about 1,500 of the 5,000 adult males living in Geneva in Rousseau's time counted as citizens, the class to which Rousseau himself was proud by birthright to belong. The others were divided into various categories, not only excluded from civil rights and privileges, but denied access to all the most lucrative trades and professions in Geneva, including watchmaking.

For reasons such as these there came to be a great deal of discontent beneath the almost utopian surface of appearances in Geneva.[9] There were citizens who opposed the domination of their republic by the patrician families, and there were non-franchised inhabitants who opposed the monopoly of rights and privileges by the citizens.[10] The movement of opposition to the patrician regime which developed among the citizens at the end of the seventeenth century was in many ways a Whiggish, or liberal, movement asserting the rights of the citizens in the General Council against usurpations of the patriciate in the Council of Twenty-Five. The leaders of this movement were themselves members of the patrician class; even so, two of them, Pierre Fatio and Nicolas Lemaître, were both put briskly to death by the government in 1707, five years before Rousseau's birth. Fatio had a following among citizens of humbler social status who lived in the lower reaches of the city. Such men were artisans,

9. G. Vallette, *J.-J. Rousseau, Genevois*, Paris, 1911.

10. It has been argued that these two centres of discontent combined to form an important popular and democratic force in eighteenth-century Geneva, based on the 'unity of the artisan class', and that Jean-Jacques Rousseau was nurtured in that intellectual environment, so that his political thought has to be understood against that background. The leading exponent of this theory is Michel Launay, who has set it out most fully in *Jean-Jacques Rousseau: Écrivain politique*, Cannes, 1971. This book owes some of its arguments to an unpublished Ph.D. thesis by Patrick O'Mara accepted by the University of California in 1952, 'Geneva in the Eighteenth Century', but in my view O'Mara's research does not bear out the conclusions that Launay draws from it. The opposition to the regime in Geneva was not as popular and democratic as Launay makes it out to be, and Rousseau was not influenced by it until the 1760s when, as author of *Émile* and *The Social Contract*, he was persecuted by the Genevan authorities.

INTRODUCTION

but they were in no way proletarian. As a result of Calvin's system of public instruction, the artisans of Geneva were educated; they could not only read, several of them possessed books by the great philosophers, historians and political theorists.[11] The typical Genevan watch-maker was '*petit-bourgeois gentilhomme*' who modelled his lifestyle on that of the Genevan patrician.[12] One such man situated between the patriciate and the unfranchised majority of inhabitants was Rousseau's paternal grandfather, David, a follower of Pierre Fatio. If we may use an anachronistic word and call Fatio's supporters 'liberals', David Rousseau is to be numbered among them. In the year 1690, after the victory of William III in the Battle of the Boyne, the 'liberals' of Geneva let off fireworks and lit bonfires in celebration; and we see from the records[13] that David Rousseau is one of those accused of lighting a bonfire too close to the house of the French Resident and of thus giving offence to France. Some years later, when the dispute between the regime and the opposition became more acute, David Rousseau was deprived of the office of *dizenier*, that is, a subaltern of the militia who was also responsible for the surveillance of the people's morals in his quarter.[14] He was hardly important enough to have been put to death with Fatio and Lemaître in 1707, but he was punished.

There is, however, no evidence to suggest that Rousseau's father Isaac shared the political sentiments of his grandfather David, and much to suggest that he had rather different opinions. At the time of the liberal agitation which culminated in the executions of 1707 Isaac Rousseau was abroad, having gone to work as a watch-maker in Constantinople in 1705. When he returned to Geneva in 1711, tranquillity had been restored, and there was little if any talk of rebellion.

One may wonder at the success of the patrician regime, but it is not unintelligible. The upper classes of Geneva did not quarrel among themselves, like those of Florence, to ruin the republic; they did not exploit the populace as did those of France; they made their fortunes

---

11. See O'Mara's thesis conserved in the Archives de l'État, Geneva.
12. See Charles Du Bois-Melly, *Les Mœurs genevoises du 1700 à 1760*, Geneva, 1882.
13. *Annales*, XVI, pp. 62–3.
14. See R. A. Leigh, *Annales*, 1979, pp. 106–7.

from foreigners, by banking and commercial activity. Taxes were not only fair, but Geneva, unlike other city-states in Europe at the time, was solvent. Besides the excellent system of public education, the regime provided unusually effective welfare arrangements, and through the *Chambre de blé* assured food at fair prices when other places suffered the effects of bad harvests. The patricians of Geneva were honest, public-spirited and cultured. Nor were they without a certain cunning in forging alliances with the disfranchised majority of inhabitants against the 1,500 citizens. Pierre Fatio and his followers might claim that the law made the General Council the sovereign body of the republic, but the patriciate could reply that the law made the republic sovereign over itself, and that the law also made the Council of Twenty-Five the supreme authority of that republic, with power to decide not only on behalf of the minority on the citizens' roll but of the city as a whole; to this extent there was a 'conservative' as well as a 'liberal' ideology in Geneva.

Rousseau's father Isaac was a socially ambitious man who fretted against the constraints of the artisan's life. He married above himself socially, so that Jean-Jacques was born, not in the artisan parish of St Gervais where his father had been born, but in the elegant quarter near the Hôtel de Ville, in his mother's house. Although Rousseau's mother, born Suzanne Bernard, was not of the social and political élite from which the rulers of Geneva were drawn, she came from the academic élite which Calvin had elevated to a position of distinction which enabled its members to meet social aristocracy on equal terms. It was Suzanne's uncle, Samuel Bernard, a prominent theologian and scholar, who had bequeathed to her the handsome house in the Grand'rue where Jean-Jacques was born and the library which served to lay the foundation of his education, unusual as that education was.

A week after Rousseau's birth, his mother, already in her fortieth year, died of puerperal fever. In an early draft of his *Confessions*, Rousseau wrote 'I cost the life of the best of mothers',[15] but in later versions he removed the hyperbole, doubtless realizing that no mother so soon dead could be the best of them. What perhaps he had done, and was certainly made to feel he had done, was to rob his father of the best of wives.

15. *J.-J.*, p. 13.

Isaac Rousseau, with his yearnings for grandeur, always wore a sword, which every citizen was authorized to do, but which other artisans seldom actually did. He preferred hunting and dancing to watch-making, and more than once engaged in duels with men of rank and station above his own. But he was no good as a breadwinner, and when Jean-Jacques was five Isaac had to sell the house in the Grand'rue and return to the artisan quarter of St Gervais, where, with the aid of his sister, he brought up his two sons.

Jean-Jacques was the favourite. Indeed the firstborn, François, was so little favoured that he soon ran away from Geneva and never communicated with his family again. Jean-Jacques has only good to say in the *Confessions* of his own upbringing: 'The children of kings could not have been more zealously cared for than I was.'[16] Isaac clearly inculcated into his son the virtues of patriotism, and gave him an idealized vision of his own country. Jean-Jacques was encouraged to see Geneva as a modern Rome.

In the *Confessions*, Rousseau says that the Roman model 'helped to create in me that free and republican spirit, that proud and strong character, impatient of any yoke, or servitude, which has tormented me all my life in situations where it has been least appropriate'.[17] For some reason he was never allowed to go to school in Geneva, but was educated at home, like Kierkegaard and John Stuart Mill, by his father. If he regretted not going to school with other boys, he never admitted it in print. He stressed rather the superiority of his education, in a family 'whose manners distinguished it from the people'.[18] His childhood was dominated by his father's ideas. Of his grandfather he has hardly a word to say, either in the *Confessions* or in his letters; indeed, when David Rousseau died at the age of ninety-five in an infirmary, he seems to have more or less been forgotten by his family.

Of his father, Jean-Jacques always spoke with veneration. For example, in his *Letter to M. D'Alembert on the Theatre* written when he was forty-five, there is an eloquent passage which reads:

I remember being struck in my childhood by a rather simple scene ... the St Gervais militia had completed their exercises and, as was the custom, each of the companies ate together; and after supper most of them met in

16. *OC*, I, p. 10.   17. *OC*, I, p. 61.   18. *OC*, I, p. 61.

the square of St Gervais, where the officers and soldiers all danced together around the fountain.

My father, embracing me, was thrilled in a way that I can still feel and share. 'Jean-Jacques', he said to me, 'love your country. Look at these good Genevans; they are all friends; They are all brothers; joy and harmony reigns among them. You are a Genevan. One day you will see other nations, but even if you travel as far as your father has, you will never find any people to match your own'.[19]

Rousseau's education at his father's knee reached its peak in studying the heroic biographies of Plutarch; and Rousseau claims, 'I was a Roman at the age of twelve'.[20] In fact, by the time he was ten, the readings from Plutarch came to an end because Isaac Rousseau had been forced to leave Geneva as a result of challenging a person of higher rank than himself to a duel, not only making a 'gentleman's' appeal to the sword, but when he was told he was no gentleman, actually wielding the sword. With Isaac Rousseau thus exiled from Geneva, and from his son's life, Jean-Jacques became the ward of his mother's brother, Colonel Bernard, under whose care he was brought up for some years with his cousin, Abraham, *en pension* with a Calvinist pastor in a village outside the city walls. All went well until the day came for the two boys to be prepared for a career: Abraham was set on the way to become an army officer like his father; Jean-Jacques was sent down the hill again to St Gervais to be a living-in apprentice with an engraver who was no *petit-bourgeois gentilhomme* but brutish, coarse and cruel.

Abraham was a boy of the fashionable quarters: I, wretched apprentice, was no more than a child of St Gervais. There was no longer equality between us, in spite of our birth; it would have been *infra dig* for him to continue our association.[21]

Like his father, Jean-Jacques had come down in the world, and, similarly, he found the situation so intolerable that he ended up by running away from Geneva. The means of escape that was open to him was to change his religion; for the Counter-Reformation was still active in the duchy of Savoy, with Catholic missionaries on the look-out for potential converts among young people who fled from the dour puritan austerity of life in Calvin's Christian commonwealth.

19. Fuchs, Lille, 1948, pp. 181–2. *Lettre à M. d'Alembert sur les spectacles*. An excellent translation of this letter is provided by Allen Bloom in *Politics and the Arts*, Glencoe, 1960.
20. *CC*, V, p. 242.   21. *OC*, I, p. 42.

INTRODUCTION

Savoy was still a more or less feudal type of society, and it was to the aristocracy of Savoy that Rousseau turned for help. He went first to the *curé* of Confignon, because (as he tells us) he knew that the *curé* was a person of blue blood; and as he wandered afterwards on foot from Confignon to Annecy, he recalls that he made his way to the walls of every noble château, dreaming of making friends with the lord and lady of the castle and winning the hand of the daughter. Rousseau says he never felt any sexual attraction to lower-class girls. He liked only those with good clothes and well-dressed hair and delicate complexions. All the working girls he speaks of in the *Confessions* are described ungraciously; and even middle-class girls seem to have left him unmoved. It is the upper-class young ladies who figure in his fantasies, his memories, his reveries.[22]

His quest for aristocratic society in Savoy and Piedmont was not unsuccessful. At Annecy he was welcomed by the Baronne de Warens, who embraced him. In Turin, the Comte de Gouvon took him into his palazzo as a footman; his son the Abbé de Gouvon promptly transformed him into his secretary, and set about teaching him to appreciate literature. Then, back in Savoy, Rousseau settled down to life with the noblewoman who became in turn his benefactress, protectress, foster-mother and mistress.

Madame de Warens was not, it is true, very highly placed in the European aristocracy. The title she bore had been bought with an estate in the *pays de Vaud* for her husband by her father-in-law at the time of her marriage; it had been alienated when her husband sold the estate after she had deserted him and ruined him financially; he had ceased to call himself the Baron de Warens. But being a baroness was an important part of the role she played in the duchy of Savoy, as an aristocratic Swiss convert to the Catholic church helping the conversion of others, supported financially in this pious work by the King of Sardinia and the Bishop of Annecy.

Madame de Warens has always had a bad press. She was something of an adventuress, and her sexual morals were not those of middle-class respectability. But she was a woman of great generosity and considerable culture; she educated Rousseau. She provided the intellectual formation which enabled him to become the writer he

22. See especially his story of the '*L'Idyle des carises*', *J.-J.*, pp. 88–91, and F. and J. Serand, *L'Idyle des carises*, Chambéry, 1928.

eventually became. She did not, however, contribute much to his political education. Her own conception of politics was a limited one. She saw politics as intrigue; and, characteristically, she tried to win further favour with the King of Sardinia by engaging in espionage. In any case, at the time he lived with Madame de Warens in Savoy – that duchy having declined into being a mere province of the Kingdom of Sardinia, governed by Italian bureaucrats and intendants – Rousseau was far removed from anything that deserved the name of politics.

After his flight from Geneva at the age of sixteen, Rousseau seldom revisited his native city. However, at the age of twenty-five, he happened to be there when the 'liberal' – or 'citizens'' – party opposition to the government reached the brink of civil war. His reaction to these events is instructive. In letters[23] he wrote at the time, he had nothing to say about the rebellion except that it was incommoding his efforts to put his hands on the inheritance from his mother which, having attained his majority under Genevan law, he was at last entitled to claim. Personal concerns drove out all others. In the *Confessions*, again, he speaks of this moment in Genevan history. He says he was particularly shocked to see his two friends, M. Barrillot, the bookseller, and his son Jacques-François coming out of the same house armed to the teeth to fight on opposite sides in the civil war 'with the prospect of cutting each other's throats'. Rousseau declares: 'This terrible sight made such a deep impression on me that I swore there and then never to take part in any civil war, and never, if I were to regain my citizenship, to struggle for liberty by taking up arms...'[24]

The civil strife in Geneva ended when both sides accepted the arbitration of foreign Mediators led by the Comte de Lautrec, and Rousseau, in his first published poem,[25] implored his countrymen to end their discord and follow the path of reconciliation.

Years later in Paris Rousseau made the acquaintance of one of the most radical members of the citizens' faction, one of the few who, refusing the terms of Lautrec's mediation, was driven into exile. This was Toussaint-Pierre Lenieps. Rousseau may have heard marsh

23. See Rousseau to Madame de Warens, July 1737 (*CC*, I, pp. 44–8).
24. *OC*, I, p. 216; *J.-J.*, p. 125.
25. *Le Verger de la Baronne de Warens*, Chambéry, 1739, p. 8.

criticisms of the political situation in Geneva from Lenieps, but if he did he was not persuaded by them at first, for letters he wrote in the early 1750s bespeak the same admiration for the Genevan government as does his Dedication of the *Discourse on Inequality*. For example, in May 1751 he told a correspondent in Geneva

> all the circumstances of my life have served to give more fire to that ardent love of country which my father inspired in me. It is as a result of living (in exile) among slaves that I have come to feel the value of liberty. How happy are you to dwell among men who obey only the laws, that is to say, Reason.[26]

Rousseau's thinking about the politics defined itself thereafter in the context of two sorts of stimulus: the experience of living in a great Kingdom and his encounter with the political views of the Enlightenment; though perhaps it is only fair to remember that he had already studied, in the library of Madame de Warens, the writings of such political philosophers as Hobbes, Locke, Pufendorf, and Burlamaqui. At the age of twenty-eight, as a private tutor in M. de Mably's house in Lyons, Rousseau became conscious of himself as a 'republican', a citizen of Geneva, a stranger in the world of monarchs and princes. A revealing document here is a poem he wrote to one of his friends in Lyons, the surgeon Parisot.

In this poem[27] Rousseau refers to himself as a man from Geneva 'born free', and brought up to know that through his birth as citizen he had the right to participate in the supreme power of his native republic as a member of its sovereign body. He then goes on to say such things as: 'I have learned to respect an illustrious nobility', and 'It would not be good in society for there to be less inequality between the ranks.'

Of course nobody is on oath in writing poetry; but these verses do give us some idea of how Rousseau reacted to his first experience of living in France, befriended by the *noblesse de robe* of Lyons. Then in Paris he met the political theory of the Encyclopaedists. Not all the Encyclopaedists, assuredly, held the same political views, but there were two main currents, the liberal constitutionalism of Montesquieu, and the doctrine that was expressed in a moderate form by Voltaire and an extreme form by the Baron d'Holbach – enlightened absolutism.

26. *CC*, II, pp. 153–5; *J.-J.*, p. 255.
27. *OC*, II, pp. 1136–46. The poem was finished on 10 July 1742.

INTRODUCTION

The Encyclopaedists were immensely influenced by Bacon – they spoke a lot about Locke, but Bacon was really their hero; and although Montesquieu continued to uphold Locke's kind of politics, the other Encyclopaedists were drawn ever closer to Bacon with his radical scheme to wipe away religion and traditional philosophy and replace it with the rule of science and technology aimed at improving the life of man on earth. Science was to be the salvation of mankind. Bacon's personal project was to make James I a king who would use his absolute powers to govern scientifically as Bacon advised him to govern; and this was the package which Voltaire, Holbach and La Rivière tried to sell such monarchs as Frederick II of Prussia and Catherine the Great of Russia.

When Rousseau first arrived in Paris in 1742 at the age of thirty with the aim of winning fame and fortune, he was caught up with his friend Diderot in this flood of Enlightenment ideology and bourgeois aspiration, only to repudiate it later as part of what he called his 'reform'. An important stage in his political education was a year he spent, between the ages of thirty-one and thirty-two, as secretary to the French Ambassador in Venice, the Comte de Montaigu. This was in many ways an unfortunate experience, but Rousseau learned much from it.

The French Ambassador was a retired brigadier with no qualifications or aptitude for diplomacy. Rousseau, who was efficient and quick, and could speak Italian, performed the duties of Embassy Secretary. It was a time when he was ambitious, yearning for what he called '*gloire*' and '*fortune*'. He bought himself expensive, elegant clothes from Paris, and fancied himself as a diplomatist, practising an aristocratic profession in the service of the greatest king in Europe. But this is not how the Ambassador regarded him; the Ambassador saw him as his personal clerk, little better than a valet. His Excellency, who was not an easy man, became incensed when Rousseau put on the airs of a fellow diplomatist, stretched himself languidly in the armchairs of the Embassy, or demanded to have the Embassy gondola at his personal disposal. There were heated words on both sides; within a year Rousseau was sacked in the most humiliating manner possible. But at least he had had time to learn how Venice was governed, and to start writing a book on political institutions, from which he extracted, to publish separately in 1762, his *Social Contract*.

Moreover, as soon as Rousseau returned to Paris his luck changed. He found a job as secretary in the family of an immensely rich tax-farmer named Dupin and lived with them in the most beautiful of all French châteaux, that at Chenonceaux. As research assistant to M. and Mme Dupin he studied the political philosophy of Montesquieu (and found himself more in agreement with Montesquieu's aristocratic outlook than with his employer's bourgeois criticisms of Montesquieu). He published works about music, composed operas and ballets, wrote plays, and even prepared one of Voltaire's works for the stage. He was indeed well on the way to achieve the *gloire* and *fortune* he hoped for as an intellectual of the Enlightenment.

He also acquired a mistress, not a beautiful woman, or an educated, upper-class one of the kind he usually admired, but a laundry-maid named Thérèse Levasseur who worked at the hotel in Paris where he lodged. Rousseau kept her, and her family, for the rest of his life; she was the mother of his five illegitimate children. 'I declared to her in advance', he tells us, 'that I would never abandon her and never marry her'.[28] He did in fact marry her when he was fifty-six but he was not prompted to do so when, aged thirty-seven, he had the 'illumination' which led him, he claimed, to 'reform' himself and alter his way of life altogether. Every reader of the *Confessions* must remember the story Rousseau tells of his walk to Vincennes to visit Diderot when Diderot was imprisoned there, and his discovering on the way an advertisement for a prize essay at Dijon on the subject of whether the revival of the arts and sciences had improved men's morals; and his realization, in a blinding flash, that such progress had in fact corrupted morals. Hardly able to breathe, let alone walk, he tells us, he sat down under a tree and wept.[29]

The result was Rousseau's *Discourse on the Sciences and the Arts*, which won the Dijon prize in 1750. Diderot encouraged Rousseau to compete, yet the *Discourse* is, in fact, a sustained attack on everything the Enlightenment stood for, and everything that the *Encyclopaedia* was intended to promote. The ideas Rousseau sets forth in his first discourse were held by others, but those others were reactionaries whereas Rousseau was an Encyclopaedist, one of Diderot's most valued contributors.

28. *OC*, I, p. 331.   29. *OC*, I, p. 1135.

INTRODUCTION

It was remarkable that a *philosophe* of the Enlightenment should make such an attack on Baconian ideas. For Rousseau claimed that science, far from saving us, was bringing ruin on mankind; progress was an illusion; the development of modern culture had made men neither happier nor more virtuous. Virtue was possible, he argued only in simple societies, where people lived austere and frugal lives; in modern, sophisticated cultures man was corrupt and the greater the sophistication the greater the corruption. Rousseau invoked the authority of Plato to support his case; for had not Plato said that all so-called scientific knowledge was not knowledge at all, and proposed that poets and artists be banished from an ideal republic?

To Diderot, a cheerful and tolerant man, all these arguments were perhaps so many entertaining paradoxes, attractive to his intellectual mind. But clearly someone who believed them seriously could not remain in the position in which Rousseau had placed himself as a young intellectual seeking fame and fortune as a member of progressive, fashionable bourgeois society in Paris. A radical change in his way of life was inevitable, especially after he had published his essay and his opinions became known. One of the first steps he took was to renounce the ambition of making a fortune, and to quit the job he had been given in the office of his rich friend, Dupin de Francueil, a job in which he might have lined his own pockets substantially. It was at this time that Rousseau must have written one of his most interesting and least known essays, his unfinished *Discours sur les richesses*.

This paper is among the manuscripts of Rousseau in the Public Library at Neuchâtel, in Switzerland, where the fragments were pieced together by a former librarian, Félix Bovet, and published by him, with some omissions, through a small Paris bookseller[30] in 1853 and only once reprinted.[31] The discourse is addressed to one Chrysophyle – who is doubtless Rousseau himself – and is designed to persuade the recipient to give up his project of making a fortune. Chrysophyle, we learn, desires to become rich only in order to have the means to do good in the world. His wealth is going to be used to relieve the sufferings of his less fortunate fellow-men. The author argues that this project is one that can never be accomplished. First, he points out that a poor man can accumulate a fortune only by saving every penny

30. Charles Reinwald, 15 rue des Saintes-Pères, Paris.
31. *Œuvres complètes*, ed. Launay, Paris, 1967, vol. II.

he acquires; he must cultivate habits of avarice, and thus, in preparing for the distant future when he will give away liberally, he must harden his heart against any kind of generosity. Secondly, when that remote day dawns and his fortune is made, the newly-rich man will no longer look upon the world from the perspective of a poor man. The poor man is sensitive to the evils of poverty precisely because he is poor himself; but once he is rich, why should he continue to feel the same way? Then again, by what means is a fortune to be made? A poor man can be honest; a man born rich can be honest; but it is not so easy to be honest while devoting one's life to the activity of getting rich, for the readiest ways of making a profit are often the least ethical ways. So Rousseau concludes that the idea of becoming rich in order to do good in the world is an impossible project, because the effort of getting rich will deprive a man of the desire to do good as soon as he acquires the power to do it.

It is important to notice that this discourse is neither an attack on hereditary wealth, nor an attack on the values of the aristocracy, but on those of the acquisitive bourgeoisie, of the people by whom Rousseau was befriended in his early years in Paris, the Dupins and the Poplinières, and on such well-off bourgeois intellectuals as Holbach and Voltaire. The reason for thinking that Rousseau addressed the discourse to himself is that he had hitherto looked upon his project of making money as one designed solely to enable him to provide material help for his old benefactress, Madame de Warens, in her years of sickness and need; he had never desired to make money for himself.

'In February, 1751', Rousseau writes in the *Confessions*, 'I renounced forever all ideas of fortune and advancement in the world'.[32] Ironically, having thus renounced all ideas of fortune, he promptly acquired enormous fame.

He owed his fame in part to his association with Diderot's *Encyclopaedia*, as chief author of the articles on music and of several contributions on other subjects. The *Encyclopaedia* itself was an immense success, so that the arrival of Rousseau on the scene coincided with that of a whole group of his friends. The intellectual, or *philosophe*, suddenly became fashionable. Voltaire, who was himself the model on which the type was based, observed in an article[33] that whereas in the

---

32. *OC*, I, p. 362.   33. *Encyclopédie*, vol. II: '*Homme de lettres*'.

early years of the century 'men of letters were not admitted to polite society, they have now become a necessary part of it'. The salons of the past had been peopled exclusively by persons of rank; now class no longer mattered. The *philosophes* came from diverse backgrounds: Helvétius, Saint-Lambert, Chastellux, Condillac, Holbach and Buffon came from various levels of the nobility; Voltaire, Diderot, Raynal, Duclos, Morellet, Marmontel from the bourgeoisie; Grimm was a German baron, d'Alembert was a foundling. All that mattered was that a man should have published something interesting, and know how to talk. The *philosophe* had not only to be intelligent, he had also to be amusing. Any subject could be talked about so long as it was discussed with wit; and in general the *philosophes* did not disappoint their hostesses and admirers. Traditional ideas, especially religious and moral ones, were the favourite targets, and established institutions, especially the Church, were still powerful and intolerant enough to warrant the mockery of men who considered themselves, above all else, humane.

Rousseau's position in this milieu was paradoxical. He lacked the polish of a conventional *homme de salon*, and sometimes felt self-consciously provincial and ill at ease; but he had also a great personal charm, a bearish, lovable simplicity which even the most exigent hostesses adored. He was greatly in demand in polite society, and for all his protests he obviously enjoyed himself more often than not among his fellow intellectuals in the salons of the fashionable rich.

His fame received a further boost when his opera *The Village Soothsayer* (*Le Devin du village*) was performed at Fontainebleau to the delight of the King and Mme de Pompadour, and afterwards in Paris, to the delight of the whole theatre-going public. With this opera, and with his writings on music, Rousseau propelled the lyrical theatre into a new direction towards romanticism, ending the classical age dominated by Rameau, and introducing the age of Mozart and Gluck.[34] The King himself wished to become Rousseau's patron as a composer, and offered him the prospect of a glittering future in the one art for which Rousseau believed he had been 'born', music.

Rousseau refused; brusquely he turned his back on the King and the

---

34. See *J.-J.*, pp. 271–91; and R. Wokler, 'Rousseau and Rameau on Revolution', in Brissenden and Eade (eds), *Studies in the Eighteenth Century*, VI, Canberra, 1979, pp. 251–83.

King's money. Diderot scolded him for irresponsibility, and undoubtedly Rousseau had put himself in a false position. How could he be at the same time both the scourge of all the arts and sciences, as he was in his prize winning *Discourse*, and an exponent of several of those arts and sciences, as a contributor to the *Encyclopaedia* and composer of *The Village Soothsayer*? His critics charged him with hypocrisy. In a preface he wrote for the printed version of his play *Narcisse*, he answered back defiantly; he said he would go on writing books, plays and music 'while at the same time saying all the ill I can about literature and those who practise it'.[35] Even so, his mind was troubled.

His disapproval of the rich made it increasingly illogical for him to lead the life of a fashionable intellectual in Paris. He expressed that disapproval both in private and in published writings. When Mme de Francueil asked him if it was true that he had sent all the children his mistress had borne him to the orphanage he answered 'Yes', and told her why: 'Nature wishes us to have children because the earth produces enough to feed everybody; it is the style of life of the rich; it is your style of life which robs my children of bread'.[36] In the preface to *Narcisse* he attacks the teaching of the fashionable economists that man's material interests generate a mutual dependence and useful commerce within society, and says that economic interests divide men rather than unite them and that men's pursuit of gain rather than duty or virtue produces nothing other than violence, perfidy and betrayal: in modern French society, 'divided as it is, between rich and poor, the rich are corrupted by their culture, and the poor are depraved by their misery: both are equally slaves of vice.'[37]

It was in the late autumn of 1753 that the Academy of Dijon announced an essay competition on the question 'What is the origin of inequality among men, and is it authorized by Natural Law?' Rousseau responded promptly: 'if the Academy had the courage to raise such a question', he decided, 'I would have the courage to write about it'.[38] Then he went to the country for a week to meditate 'in solitude' on what he was to say. He was not in fact entirely alone, for Thérèse and two other women went with him to take care of him and prepare his meals; but he spent the days walking by himself

35. *OC*, II, p. 974. 36. *CC*, IX, pp. 14–18; *J.-J.*, p. 244.
37. *OC*, II, p. 969. 38. *OC*, I, p. 388.

in the forest of Saint-Germain, and it was there, he tells us, under the trees in an unusually sunny November, that he first reflected on what the life of men must have been like before civilizations had been introduced:

> There I sought, and there I found, the image of that early time of which I had afterwards the temerity to write the history ... I dared to strip man's nature naked, to follow the evolution of those times and things which have disfigured him; I compared man-made man with natural man, and I discovered that his supposed improvement had generated all his miseries.[39]

In short, developing the view put forward in his other early writings about the decay of culture, Rousseau now set out to show that both nature and natural man were good. 'Out of these meditations', he says, 'there emerged the *Discourse on Inequality*.'[40]

Rousseau finished the *Discourse* when he got back to Paris, wandering in the Bois de Boulogne to think, then hurrying home to write down his thoughts. The result was an essay which is remarkable both as philosophy and science. In less than a hundred pages, Rousseau outlined a theory of the evolution of the human race which prefigured the discoveries of Darwin; he revolutionized the study of anthropology and linguistics, and he made a seminal contribution to political and social thought. Even if his argument was seldom fully understood by his readers, it altered people's ways of thinking about themselves and about their world; it even changed their ways of feeling. Of all his writings, Rousseau's *Discourse on Inequality* – often referred to as his *Second Discourse* – has perhaps been the most influential. The books of his later years – *Émile, The Social Contract, Confessions* and *La Nouvelle Héloïse* – are more 'substantial', but it is as the author of the second *Discourse* that Rousseau has both been held responsible for the French Revolution and acclaimed as the founder of modern social science. It is the masterpiece of his early years, although it did not, as did his first *Discourse*, win the prize at Dijon.[41]

He begins his inquiry by noting that there are two kinds of inequality among men. The first are natural inequalities, arising from differences in strength, intelligence, agility and so forth; the second

---

39. *OC*, I, p. 389. 40. *ibid.*
41. One reason for Rousseau's failure to win the prize may be that his identity became known in Dijon before the winner was announced in July, 1754 (see R. Tisserand, *Les Concurrents de Rousseau à Dijon*, Paris, 1936, pp. 13–14).

are artificial inequalities, which derive from the conventions which govern society. Rousseau suggests that it is because of these artificial inequalities that some men are richer than others, some more honoured than others, and some obeyed by others. He takes the main problem of his discourse to be to explain the origins of such artificial inequalities, since there would be no point in asking why nature had come to bestow its gifts unequally. He therefore sees his first duty as that of distinguishing what is properly and originally natural to man from what man has made for himself. This Rousseau thinks can only be done by going back in time to ascertain what man was like before civilizations were introduced. The way to learn about natural man is to rediscover original man. Although Rousseau allows that men have been related to orang-outangs, he does not hold the view later taken by Darwin that man has evolved from cousins of the apes; he does suggest that man developed from a very primitive biped into the sophisticated creature of modernity, and that the evolution can be largely understood as a process of adaptation and struggle.

Rousseau does not claim to be the first to try to explain human society by referring to a pre-social 'state of nature'; he only argues that earlier thinkers, such as Hobbes and Locke, have simply not been scientific enough:

> Philosophers who have examined the foundations of society have all felt it necessary to go back to the state of nature, only none of them has succeeded in getting there; all of them, talking ceaselessly about 'need', 'greed', 'oppression', 'desire' and 'pride', have transported into the state of nature concepts formed in society; they speak of savage man, but they depict civilized man.

The philosopher whom Rousseau has most in mind here is Hobbes. In Hobbes the state of nature is represented as one of war of each man against all men; human beings are seen as aggressive, avaricious, proud, selfish and afraid; and on the basis of this picture of natural man Hobbes goes on to claim that without the mortal solicitude of a civil ruler, men's lives would be 'solitary, poor, nasty, brutish and short'.[42] Rousseau asserts, against Hobbes, that all the unpleasant characteristics of the human condition derive not from nature but from society; and that if we look back far enough in our search for

---

42. *Leviathan*, I, chap. 13, §11.

the origins of man, we shall find a being who is admittedly solitary, but healthy, happy, good and free.

Rousseau envisages earliest man as a being removed only to a limited extent from the life of a beast, 'an animal less strong than some, less agile than others, but, taken as a whole, the most advantageously organized of all'. Natural man is not complicated. 'I see him satisfying his hunger under an oak, quenching his thirst at the first stream, finding his bed under the same tree which has furnished his meal; and behold his needs are satisfied.'

In claiming that original man had a sound constitution Rousseau contrasts the health of savages, as observed by travellers, with the diseases which afflict men in modern society, where the rich are overfed and the poor underfed, and everyone is harassed by the wants, fatigues, anxieties, excesses, passions and sorrows which civilization generates. Domesticated men, like domesticated animals, says Rousseau, become effeminate. In the state of nature, men are fit, if only because they have to be fit to survive.

Accustomed from childhood to the inclemencies of the weather, and the rigour of the seasons, to overcoming fatigue, and forced to defend themselves and their prey naked and unarmed against other wild beasts, or to escape from such beasts by running faster, men develop a robust and almost unvarying temperament. Children, coming into the world with the excellent constitution of their fathers, and strengthening it by the same exercise which produced it, thus acquire all the vigour of which the human race is capable. Nature treats them precisely as the laws of Sparta treated the children of its citizens; it makes those who are already well constituted strong and robust, and it makes all the others die.

Yet while Rousseau identifies natural man to a large extent with original man and sees no great difference between the life of original man and that of a beast, he nevertheless regards man as a unique species, unique among animals, that is, in possessing freedom and a capacity for self-improvement. Both these defining characteristics of man need some explanation.

Natural man is free, for Rousseau, in three senses of the word 'freedom'. First he has free will. This is a crucial sense for Rousseau. Hobbes and most of the *encyclopédistes* were determinists, believing that man was a 'machine', albeit more complicated than any other machine in nature, but subject to the same laws of cause and effect.

While it is true that Rousseau himself invokes the metaphor of a machine in describing living creatures, he stresses the fact that the 'human machine' differs from the 'animal machine' in being autonomous; among beasts, nature alone 'operates the machine'; in the case of a human being, the individual contributes to his own operations in the capacity of a free agent. 'The beast chooses and rejects by instinct; man by an act of free will.'

This metaphysical freedom, or freedom of the will, as a defining characteristic of man as such is possessed by men in all conditions, whether of nature or of society. But there are two other forms of freedom which men had, according to Rousseau, in the state of nature; one is anarchic freedom and the other personal freedom. The anarchic freedom was, of course, absolute, since by definition the 'state of nature' is a condition where there is no government and no positive law. When Rousseau came some years later to write the *Social Contract*, he condemned anarchic freedom with almost the same fervour as did Hobbes; but only to exalt the idea of 'freedom under law' as an alternative to Hobbes's recipe of absolute sovereignty. In Rousseau's *Second Discourse*, by contrast, pre-political freedom, though absolute, is depicted as a happy enough condition precisely because original man is not seen by Rousseau, as he is seen by Hobbes, as an aggressive creature, but rather as a harmless solitary being who, having no experience of society, has no need of political regulation.

The third form of freedom enjoyed by man in a state of nature, according to Rousseau, is the one to which he assigns the highest importance and value, personal freedom in the sense of having no master, no employer, no immediate superior: original man is not dependent on anyone else for his livelihood. Speaking of the state of nature, Rousseau puts this question:

> Is there a man who is so much stronger than me, and who is moreover depraved enough, lazy enough and fierce enough to compel me to provide for his sustenance while he remains idle? He must resolve not to lose sight of me for a single moment ... for fear that I should escape or kill him.[43]

Original man is economically independent, and it is hardly surprising that Rousseau, with his own bitter memories of a lifetime of economic dependence, should emphasize this kind of personal freedom

43. *OC*, III, p. 161.

(the absence of masters or employers) which, together with anarchic freedom (the absence of civil rules and rulers), distinguishes the life of men in a state of nature.

Besides having *liberté* (in these several senses) original man, as Rousseau sees him, differed from beasts in possessing *perfectibilité*, or the capacity for self-improvement. This was a characteristic of man which other theorists of the Enlightenment emphasized. It was indeed most emphasized by those who expounded the doctrine of progress which Rousseau had attacked in his *Discourse on the Sciences and the Arts*. Turgot, for example, had some four years earlier given a lecture at the Sorbonne, 'The Successive Advances of the Human Mind', in which he 'contrasted man, equipped with this instinct of self-improvement and enabled to conserve in his culture each fresh advancement of mind, with the sub-human organic creatures, each generation of which is obliged to start at exactly the same place occupied by each preceding generation'.[44] However, this faculty of self-improvement in man which Turgot and the other ideologues of progress considered wholly beneficial, Rousseau saw as a faculty no less for self-destruction. Just as man's first defining characteristic, his freedom of choice, enabled him to choose either good or evil, so this second defining characteristic, his *'perfectibilité'* – which means not at all a potentiality for perfection, but simply a capacity for self-betterment – was equally a faculty which could be turned in the wrong direction and carry men towards the worse. This latter is what Rousseau believed had actually happened when men had reached a certain stage in their evolution; and he sets out to explain how this unhappy outcome occurred.

Original men, or 'savages' as Rousseau sometimes chooses to call our forebears as they lived in the first state of nature, were simple beings, with no language, very little capacity for thought, with few needs and, in consequence, few passions: 'since savage man desires only the things which he knows and knows only the things of which the possession is either within his power or easily obtained, then nothing ought to be so tranquil as his soul or so limited as his mind'.[45] For such an uncomplicated being, 'willing and not willing, desiring and fearing will be almost the only operations of his soul'.[46] Even

44. See R. Nisbet, *History of the Idea of Progress*, New York, 1980, p. 243.
45. *OC*, III, p. 214.   46. *OC*, III, p. 143.

the fears of such a being are limited to apprehension of known danger. A savage can fear pain but not death, because he has no concept of death; anxiety, that disease of the imagination, is unknown to him.

Conceptual thinking, Rousseau suggests, developed only with speech. Even so, he holds against certain other theorists that some primitive kind of thinking must have preceded the birth of languages. Man in the first state of nature needed to think, but he needed no language,

> having neither houses nor huts, nor any kind of property, everyone slept where he chanced to find himself, and often for one night only; males and females united fortuitously, according to encounters, opportunities and desires. They required no speech to express the things they had to say to each other; and they separated with the same ease.[47]

Here we have a denial of the view that the family is a natural society; and in a long footnote Rousseau offers a detailed criticism of Locke's suggestion that nature itself impels human males and females to unite on a more or less settled basis to feed and shelter their young. Rousseau agrees with Locke that a man may have a motive for remaining with one woman when she has a child, but he protests that Locke fails to prove that a man must remain with one woman during the nine months of pregnancy:

> For it is not a question of knowing why a man should be attached to her after she has given birth, but why he should stay with her after her conception. His appetite satisfied, the man has no longer any need of the woman, nor the woman of one particular man. The man has not the least care, and perhaps not the least idea of the effects of his action. He goes off in one direction, she in another, and there is no likelihood at the end of nine months that either will have any memory of having known the other.[48]

The point Rousseau insists upon here is that while it is undoubtedly advantageous to the human race that there should be permanent unions between males and females, 'it does not follow that such unions are established by nature'.[49] Strangely enough, in his other writings, Rousseau himself asserts that the family is a natural society. Not only does he do so in *The Social Contract* which he published several years later, but in the *Essay on the Origins of Languages* he says 'in the earliest

47. *OC*, III, p. 147. 48 *OC*, III, p. 217. 49. *OC*, III, p. 216.

time men ... had no other society than the family'[50] and even in a later section of the *Second Discourse* we find Rousseau writing: 'By the law of nature the father is master of the child for only so long as his care is necessary to him.'[51] However, in the last quotation Rousseau is doubtless referring to 'the law of nature' in the sense of that 'natural law' which governs, or ought to govern, the conduct of man, not the natural laws which are recorded by scientists. What he is plainly seeking to argue in his *Second Discourse* is that the family is a creation of human will and agreement and not of human instinct; and he dates the institution of the family from that period of evolution which he calls 'nascent society', and not from the original 'state of nature' in which individuals lead solitary lives.

Rousseau says he will leave unsolved the problem of 'which was more necessary, previously formed society for the institution of languages, or previously invented languages for the establishment of society',[52] and he limits himself to repeating briskly what he argues at length in the *Essay on the Origins of Languages* – that men's first words were natural cries. General ideas came into men's minds with the aid of abstract words, so that the development of language itself helped to create the difficulties with which civilized man torments himself. The savage, living by instinct, has no moral problems; he has no ideas of right and wrong. In the state of nature man is good; but there is no question of his being virtuous or vicious. He is happy, free, innocent; and that is all.

> One could say that savages are not wicked precisely because they do not know what it is to be good, for it is neither the development of intelligence nor the restraints of laws, but the calm of the passions and their ignorance of vice which prevents them from doing evil.[53]

There is here in Rousseau the germ of an idea developed more fully by his contemporary David Hume, namely the idea that all men's actions are prompted by passions and that while calm passions generate good conduct, violent passions drive men to do harm to themselves and to others. Rousseau wishes to emphasize that men's passions in the state of nature are both calm and few in number, and therefore

---

50. *Essai*, ed. Porset, p. 91. (This passage was almost certainly added at a later date).
51. *OC*, III, p. 182.   52. *OC*, III, p. 151.
53. *OC*, III, p. 154.

harmless, whereas society, which both multiplies and intensifies men's passions, corrupts men morally.

The savage has one sentiment or disposition which Rousseau is prompted to call 'a natural virtue' and that is compassion or pity. Rousseau suggests that this virtue can be witnessed even in animals, not only in the tenderness of mothers for their young, but in 'the aversion of horses against trampling on any living body'.[54] He suggests that this natural sentiment of pity is the source of the most important social virtues, such as kindness, generosity, mercy and humaneness. Unfortunately, Rousseau observes, these virtues are seldom found in the modern world, because modern men have become so far removed from their own natural feelings; and Rousseau cannot let pass the opportunity at this point of chastizing modern culture and its rationalistic philosophy:

> In fact pity becomes all the more intense as the perceiving animal identifies itself more intimately with the suffering animal. Now it is clear that this identification must have been infinitely closer in the state of nature than in the state of reason. It is reason which breeds pride and reflection which fortifies it; reason which turns man inward into himself.[55]

In the modern world it is the least educated people, the ones in whom the power of reasoning is least developed who, according to Rousseau, exhibit towards their suffering fellows the most lively commiseration.

Earlier theorists who had spoken of a 'state of nature' in contrast with 'civil society' had nothing to say about the history of man's passage from one condition to the other, if only because for them the 'state of nature' was generally a fiction, an intellectual construction achieved in the mind by stripping the human condition of everything it owed to the civil order. But Rousseau, writing as an evolutionist, had perforce to explain how men had come to leave the savage state.

His suggestion is that men passed by stages from the original state of nature into what he calls 'nascent society', a process that evolved over a very long stretch of time. Although Rousseau is not always as clear in his exposition as the reader might wish, he locates as the central feature of this stage the institution of settled domiciles or 'huts'. Having a home facilitated the co-habitation of males and females on a more or less permanent basis, and so introduced the family. From

---

54. *ibid.* 55. *OC*, III, pp. 155–6.

Rousseau's point of view, this innovation signalled men's departure from the true state of nature, where the individual was solitary and sexually promiscuous, and his initiation into a primitive social state.

Rousseau speaks of this passage of man from the state of nature to 'nascent society' as 'the epoch of a first revolution which established and differentiated families' and which introduced 'property of a sort'.[56] This 'property of a sort' must, however, be distinguished from the full concept of property, which emerges only after a further revolution. All that man has in 'nascent society' is a feeling of possession of the hut he occupies. This feeling may have 'produced many quarrels and fights', but, Rousseau adds, 'since the strongest men were probably the first ones to build huts which they felt themselves able to defend, it is reasonable to believe that the weak found it quicker and safer to imitate them rather than to try to dislodge them, and to have abstained from attempting to dispossess them from fear of blows rather than from any respect for ownership'.[57] The concept of a right to property came into being only with the invention of agriculture. 'Nascent society' is the period of human history which Rousseau regards as the nearest to the ideal, but he does not describe it in detail, nor even does he say enough to make his admiration for it fully intelligible to the reader.

Eloquence at this stage takes the place of reasoned argument. Rousseau describes man in 'nascent society' as being both gentler and more loving than he had been in the state of nature: for no longer did men and women copulate casually and go their separate ways indifferent to each other's fates; settled homes produced settled relationships: 'The first movements of the heart were the effect of this new situation, which united in a common dwelling husbands and wives, fathers and children.'[58] The habit of living together gave birth to the noblest sentiments known to man, namely conjugal love and (Rousseau does not hesitate to add) paternal love. 'Each family became a little society all the better united because mutual affection and liberty were its only bonds.'[59]

Man in 'nascent society' was no longer alone nor was he yet the enemy of his fellow creatures. Midway between 'the stupidity of brutes and the disastrous enlightenment of civil man', he was 'restrained by natural pity from harming anyone'.[60] It was the golden mean between the

56. OC, III, p. 167. 57. ibid. 58. OC, III, p. 168. 59. ibid. 60. OC, III, p. 170.

'indolence of the primitive state of nature' and 'the petulant activity of our own pride'; it was the time 'when there were no laws but only the terror of vengeance to restrain men';[61] and altogether it was the best time men have ever known: 'the true youth of the world and all subsequent progress has been so many steps in appearance towards the improvement of the individual, but so many steps in reality towards the decrepitude of the human race'.[62]

The reader is bound to ask why, if the primitive condition of 'nascent society' was so ideal, did men leave it? In the *Essay on the Origins of Languages* Rousseau suggests that primitive men were driven to organize more developed societies as a result of 'natural disasters, such as floods, eruptions of volcanoes, earthquakes and great fires',[63] which forced them to unite for mutual aid in common distress. Finding it difficult to understand how 'men could spontaneously renounce the happiness of their primitive freedom', Rousseau speaks of 'historical accidents' or what Professor Polin[64] calls a 'miracle' to explain their 'catastrophic passage to a condition of unhappiness'. In the *Second Discourse* Rousseau provides an alternative explanation for the development of organized society: economic shortage. As the number of persons on the earth increased, the natural abundance of provisions diminished; the individual could not feed himself on the herbs he could find, so he had to unite with others to overcome scarcity by hunting game in groups and by other such collective activities.

It was then that men moved, Rousseau suggests, from 'nascent society' to a more developed but still pre-political society. Social changes produced important moral and psychological changes in the individuals. Ceasing to be a solitary person, man not only became gentler and more affectionate in the context of the family, he became more egoistic and more corrupt in the milieu of society.

Even within the family, the human race is seen moving away from nature. Differences between the sexes increased as the women became sedentary in the home and the men became ever more active as they moved around to find food, gradually learning as their numbers created shortages to augment their natural diet of herbs with new and less natural forms of nutrition, including meat. As men began to collect and enjoy in their homes more refined commodities, they began to

61. *OC*, III, p. 171. 62. *ibid*. 63. *Essai*, p. 113.
64. R. Polin, *La Politique de la solitude*, Paris, 1971.

develop 'needs', that is, an attachment to things of which the 'loss became much more cruel than the possession of them was sweet'.[65]

Language, too, developed with the demand for communication, first between members of the same family then between neighbours, and communication between neighbours led in time to the formation of communities. At this point

> people became accustomed to judging different objects and to making comparisons; they acquire gradually ideas of merit and of beauty, which in turn produce feelings of preference. As a result of seeing each other people cannot do without seeing more of each other. A tender and sweet sentiment insinuates itself into the soul; and at the least obstacle becomes an inflamed fury; jealousy awakens with love; discord triumphs and the gentlest of passions receives the sacrifice of human blood.[66]

As ideas and sentiments were cultivated, the human race became more sociable. People met in front of their huts or under a tree; singing and dancing became their amusements; and everyone looked at the others, knowing that others looked at him. Each wanted to excel in his neighbours' eyes.

> He who sang or danced the best, he who was the most handsome, the strongest, the most adroit or the most eloquent became the most highly regarded; and this was the first step towards inequality and, at the same time, towards vice.[67]

Men began to base their conception of themselves on what other people thought of them. The idea of 'consideration' entered their minds; each wanted respect, indeed demanded respect as a right. The duties of civility emerged even among savages: a man who was wounded in his pride was even more offended than one who was wounded in his body; and each 'punished the contempt another showed him in proportion to the esteem he accorded himself'.[68] Man's corruption is the result of his being 'denatured'. In the state of nature man had what Rousseau calls *amour de soi-même*, which I have translated as 'self-love', an instinctive self-protective, self-regarding disposition which animated his efforts to stay alive, enjoy life and avoid injuries. In society this *amour de soi-même* was transformed into what Rousseau calls *amour-propre* which I have translated as 'pride'; it is the desire to be superior to others and be admired by them:

65. *OC*, III, p. 168. 66. *OC*, III, p. 169.
67. *OC*, III, pp. 169–70. 68. *OC*, III, p. 170.

> *Amour-propre* and *amour de soi-même* must not be confused; two passions very different in their nature and in their effects. *Amour de soi-même* is a natural sentiment which prompts every animal to watch over its own conservation, and which, directed in man by reason and modified by pity, produces humanity and virtue. *Amour-propre* is only a relative, artificial sentiment, born in society, prompting every individual to attach more importance to himself than to anyone else and inspiring all the injuries men do to themselves and to others; it is the true source of honour.[69]

Here, then, is what Rousseau sees as the beginning of artificial inequality among men: the desire to be better than others and the desire to be esteemed by others. Such inequality already emerges with those communities or pre-political societies which Rousseau calls 'nations' – that is, groups 'united by custom and character rather than by regulation and laws, groups having the same style of living and eating and the common influence of climate'.[70] In the early stages of society, inequalities were limited and tolerable. They became ruinous when men introduced agriculture, the use of iron and the division of labour, which Rousseau depicts as a further 'revolutionary' innovation in the experience of mankind:

> As long as men applied themselves only to work that one person could accomplish alone and to activities which did not require the collaboration of several hands, they lived as free, healthy, good and happy as they could be according to their nature; and they continued to enjoy among themselves the sweetness of independent intercourse. But from the moment that one man needed the help of another, and it was realized that it would be useful for one man to have provisions enough for two, equality disappeared; property was introduced, work became necessary and the vast forests were transformed into pleasant fields which had to be watered with the sweat of men, and in which slavery and misery were soon seen to germinate and flourish with the crops.[71]

Agriculture, then, together with metallurgy, led to those unequal master–servant relationships which Rousseau saw as most inimical to freedom and to nature: 'It is iron and wheat which first civilized men and ruined the human race.'[72] As Rousseau reconstructs the past, the division of labour began between smiths, forging tools, and farmers cultivating the land to produce food for both. The cultivation of land entailed claims being made for rightful ownership of the piece of land

69. *OC*, III, p. 219. 70. *OC*, III, p. 169. 71. *OC*, III, p. 171. 72. *ibid.*

that a particular farmer had cultivated, and this introduced the 'fatal' concept of property.

Things in this stage might have remained equal, if talents had been equal, and if, for example, the use of iron and the consumption of foodstuffs had always exactly balanced each other; but this equilibrium which nothing maintained was soon broken.[73]

The differences in men's capacities and in their circumstances produced even greater inequalities in men's conditions, which in turn led to a war between each and all.

At this point, Rousseau's argument is like Hobbes's. Indeed, while Rousseau rejects Hobbes's claim that the state of nature is a state of war between each and all, he gives a Hobbesian picture of the state of society as it was before the introduction, by a 'social contract', of political institutions. One great difference between Rousseau and Hobbes is that Rousseau argues, in the *Second Discourse*, that a social condition and not a state of nature immediately preceded the introduction of a civil order. Rousseau, as we have seen, claims that the state of nature existed, that it was peaceful and innocent, and that it was after the introduction of society that men were led to institute governments and laws because society itself ceased to be peaceful. 'Nascent society', writes Rousseau, 'gave way to the most horrible state of war.'[74]

This state of war in pre-political society as seen by Rousseau is also rather different from the war between aggressive individuals depicted by Hobbes in his account of the state of nature. Hobbes speaks of a war between equals; Rousseau sees a war provoked by inequality; by 'the usurpations of the rich and the brigandage of the poor'.[75] War begins in society when the idea of property is born and one man claims as his own what another man's hunger prompts him to seize; and when one man has to fight to get what he needs while the other man must fight to keep what he has. For Hobbes war springs from natural aggressiveness; for Rousseau war first began with the unequal division of possessions in the context of scarcity, coupled with a corruption of the human passions which was the work of culture rather than of nature.

Both Hobbes and Rousseau conceive of men finding the same remedy for the state of war among them: namely a social contract;

73. *OC*, III, p. 174.   74. *OC*, III, p. 176.   75. *ibid.*

both philosophers see as the rational alternative to the violence and destructiveness of anarchy, the institution by common agreement of a system of positive law which all must obey. But whereas Hobbes's social contract is a rational and just solution equally advantageous to all, Rousseau's social contract as it is described in his *Discourse on Inequality* is a largely fraudulent contract imposed on the poor by the rich. In the book he called *The Social Contract* Rousseau was later to depict a just covenant of a kind to which all might subscribe so as to combine liberty with law, but in the present *Discourse*, where he is writing about what actually happened – or 'must have happened' – in the past, he describes a social contract that marked the passage from anarchic society to political society in human evolution. Here, Rousseau imagines the first founder of civil institutions as a rich man saying to the poor: 'Let us unite ... let us institute rules of justice ... instead of directing our forces against each other let us unite them in one supreme power which shall govern us according to wise laws.'[76] The poor, who can appreciate that peace is better than war for everyone, agree: they do not fully see that in setting up a system of positive law they are transforming existing possessions into permanent legal property, and so perpetuating their own poverty as well as the wealth of the rich. Hence, as Rousseau puts it, 'All ran towards their chains, believing that they were securing their liberty, for although they had reason enough to discern the advantages of a civil order, they did not have experience enough to foresee the dangers.'[77]

We may notice that in his description of the 'fraudulent social contract' Rousseau always speaks of the rich dominating and deceiving the poor, not of the strong dominating and intimidating the weak. It is the economic inequality which arises from some men having assured possessions and others having nothing which Rousseau identifies as the central evil:

> The first man who having enclosed a piece of land thought of saying 'This is mine' and found people simple enough to believe him was the true founder of civil society. How many crimes, wars, murders, how much misery and horror the human race would have been spared if someone had pulled up the stakes and filled in the ditch and cried out to his fellow men: 'Beware of this impostor: you are lost if you forget that the fruits of the earth belong to everyone and that the earth itself belongs to no one.'[78]

76. *OC*, III, p. 177.   77. *OC*, III, p. 178.   78. *OC*, III, p. 164.

Of course Rousseau knew that the past could not be undone. He was not recommending anyone to go back to 'nascent society' or to primitive anarchism: he was a philosopher who deplored the choices men had once made; he nowhere suggested, as did some socialist theorists, that the same choices could be made all over again at the present time. On the contrary, Rousseau insisted that pre-political societies belonged to a past that was exceedingly remote in Europe and Asia; and he went on to argue that political societies had gone through further stages of evolution, altering with time no less than had pre-political societies.

Political societies began with the institution of government and rulers; the power thus conferred on magistrates led to the division of men into weak and strong. In the next stage, legitimate power was converted into arbitrary power, and this produced the division of men into masters and slaves. Although Rousseau does not go into details, he obviously sees the degeneration of political systems from primitive government into absolute despotism as the continuation of the pre-political degeneration of the human animal from natural man to social man. Unfortunately, political society did nothing to arrest the moral corruption of the individual. It ended the war of each against all by establishing an unjust form of peace initiated by the rich, a peace which failed in the end to do any real good to anyone, even the rich. It failed because social man cannot be happy. The savage, Rousseau suggests, has only to eat and he is at peace with nature, 'and the friend of all his fellow men'. Even if a savage has to fight with his neighbour for a meal, it will be a short struggle; 'as pride does not enter into the fight, it is ended with a few fisticuffs; the victor eats, the vanquished goes off to seek better luck elsewhere and all are pacified'.[79] In the case of social man, it is another story altogether: 'first of all it is a matter of providing necessities, then providing the extras; afterwards come the luxuries, then riches; then subjects, then slaves – he does not have a moment of respite'.[80] As men's needs become less natural, the desire to satisfy them becomes more impassioned, so that social man is never content: he will 'cut every throat until he is master of the whole universe'.[81]

This is why civil society, according to Rousseau, provides happiness neither for the rich nor for the poor:

79. *OC*, III, p. 203.   80. *ibid.*   81. *ibid.*

> Men are wicked [he writes], melancholy and constant experience removes any need for proof; yet man is naturally good; I believe I have demonstrated it. What then can have depraved him to this point if it is not the changes that have taken place in his constitution, the progress he has made and the knowledge he has acquired?[82]

Society, says Rousseau, necessarily leads men to hate one another in proportion to the conflict between their interests, so that while appearing to render services to each other, men in reality seek to do each other every imaginable harm.

Once again, Rousseau stresses the fatal role of *amour-propre* in the life of social man; the role is not unlike that played by pride and vainglory in Hobbes's picture of natural man. For both philosophers, the psychological, or moral, causes of human conflict are much the same, the main difference being that Hobbes regards the egocentricity of men as a product of nature, while Rousseau insists that it is the product of society. Indeed, Rousseau sees this same *amour-propre* at work as a motor impelling men to develop their culture; the kind of progress which he had condemned in his *Discourse on the Sciences and the Arts* he describes in the *Discourse on Inequality* as being generated by the energies of egocentric man. Ambition, a product of *amour-propre*, impels men at the same time to their greatest achievements and to their greatest misery.

> If this were the place to go into details [he continues], I would observe to what extent this universal desire for reputation, honours and promotion which devours us all, activates and compares talents and strengths, how it excites and multiplies passions, how in making all men competitors, rivals or rather enemies, it causes every day failures, successes and catastrophes of every sort by making so many contenders run the same course; I would show that this burning desire to be talked about, this yearning for distinction, which almost always keeps us in a restless state, is responsible for what is best and worst among men, for our virtues and our vices, for our sciences and our mistakes, for our conquerors and our philosophers; responsible, in short, for a multitude of bad things and a very few good ones.[83]

Rousseau here touches on a theme which was to inform much of his later thinking: the distinction between reality and appearance. Unlike Machiavelli, whom he greatly admired, he regarded the realm

---

82. *OC*, III, p. 202. 83. *OC*, III, pp. 188–9.

of appearance as the realm of falsehood. In his role as a lover of truth, Rousseau insisted more and more on the need to banish all the veils and disguises and distortions in order to uncover that reality which alone was true. This policy was to prompt him not only to reject the life of the salons but, according to his own grim logic, to repudiate also the theatre as an institution dedicated to fictions and pretence, and thus to falsehood. This more radical extension of his argument came several years later. In the *Discourse on Inequality*, attacking civilization on a broad front, he does not single out particular elements in civilization for detailed indictment. He sees the growth of inequality as one feature of a larger process: the alienation of man. The tragedy of man is that he can no longer find happiness in the only way it can be found, that is, in living according to his nature. Natural man enjoys repose and freedom; natural man is content to be idle and alone. Civilized man, on the contrary, is always active, always working, always playing a part, sometimes bowing to greater men, whom he hates, or to richer men, whom he scorns; always willing to do anything for honours, power and reputation, and yet never having enough. 'The savage lives within himself; social man always lives outside himself; he knows how to live only in the opinion of others, and it is, so to speak, from their judgement alone that he derives the sense of his own existence.'[84]

Rousseau ends the *Discourse on Inequality* by repeating his claim that this essentially false way of life – this system of judging everything by appearances and never by reality – is not 'the original state of man', but is the result of 'the spirit of society and the inequality which it engenders';[85] it is those factors which have changed and distorted all our natural inclinations.

As an indictment of human civilization Rousseau's second *Discourse* is both more radical and more disturbing than his first. It could not be expected to appeal to conservatives, as did his earlier attack on progress, and it was bound to shock liberals. Voltaire was scandalized: 'I have received, Monsieur, your new book against the human race, and I thank you', he wrote to Rousseau after he had sent him a copy. 'No one has employed so much intelligence to turn us men into beasts. One starts wanting to walk on all fours after reading your book.

---

84. *OC*, III, p. 193.   85. *OC*, III, pp. 193–4.

However, in more than sixty years I have lost the habit.'[86] Voltaire already full of criticism of Rousseau's *Discourse on the Sciences and the Arts* was in no mood to enjoy his *Discourse on Inequality*, and his marginal notes on his copy of the text conserved in Leningrad[87] betray even more antipathy than does his letter to the author, where polite compliments moderate the barbed wit. Forty of his forty-one marginal notes are hostile to Rousseau. Diderot, on the other hand, was sympathetic to Rousseau's argument, and indeed gave him some considerable help in preparing his text. This may be seen in part as evidence of Diderot's love of paradoxes, but it must also be remembered that Diderot's political views at this time were not the same as Voltaire's; he certainly did not share Voltaire's desire to protect the class interests of the property-owning bourgeoisie. Voltaire had made a great deal of money, and was proud of it; while he hated the aristocracy, he was profoundly attached to the rights of property. In the margin of his copy of Rousseau's *Second Discourse* Voltaire wrote against the paragraph where Rousseau said the first man to enclose land was the founder both of civil society and human misery: 'Behold the philosophy of a beggar who would have the rich robbed by the poor.'[88] Diderot, scraping a living as an intellectual journalist, had no such solicitude for the rights of property; he was affected rather by the sufferings of the poor. Indeed we find Diderot writing about this time such comments as these:

> The appetites of the rich are no different from the appetites of the poor ... but for the health and happiness of both, it would perhaps be better to put the poor on the diet of the rich and the rich on the diet of the poor. As it is, the idle man stuffs himself with succulent dishes, while the working man eats bread and water, and each dies before his natural term, the one from indigestion, the other from malnutrition.[89]

Taken all in all, the *Discourse on Inequality* was Rousseau's most distinctly *scientific* work, the one closest to the mainstream of Enlightenment thinking; and however much it antagonized Voltaire for political reasons, it is understandable that Diderot, judging it on

86. *OC*, III, pp. 1379–81.
87. Published in G. R. Havens, *Voltaire's Marginalia on the Pages of Rousseau*, Columbus, Ohio, and reproduced in the footnotes of the present translation.
88. Havens, p. 15.
89. Assézat–Tourneux (eds), *Œuvres complètes de Diderot*, Paris, 1875–7, II, p. 431.

INTRODUCTION

philosophical grounds, should welcome it. For here, more than anywhere else, Rousseau writes as a scientist; and here, too, he sets forth at least one principle which was central to the ideology of the Enlightenment: man's natural goodness.

Before Rousseau, as a recent historian has written, the prevailing conception of natural man was of 'someone who was compelled to live outside the human community. And all such society-less creations were something less than human, for they had cut themselves off from the means which God has granted to every man that he might achieve his end, his *telos*.'[90] For the eighteenth-century Enlightenment 'natural man' was someone whose mind was 'unfettered by the moral and intellectual constraints of civil society' and could easily be better than civilized men. Rousseau was,[6] if not the first to adumbrate, at any rate the one who most completely and effectively impressed this conception of natural man on people's minds'.[91]

Diderot himself, in some of his writings, paints an even more idealized portrait of natural man than does Rousseau; but one must remember that Diderot's *Supplément au voyage de Bougainville* was written many years later[92] than Rousseau's *Discourse on Inequality*, and that Diderot depicts natural man as corrupted by Christianity, whereas Rousseau depicts natural man as corrupted by society; Diderot is to this extent at least, a more polemical writer than Rousseau. Rousseau said different things at different times about Diderot's attitude to his *Discourse on Inequality*. In the text of his *Confessions* he writes 'the *Discourse on Inequality* was a work more to Diderot's taste than any other of my writings, and for which his advice was most useful to me.'[93] In a footnote added later, Rousseau wrote: 'Diderot always abused my confidence in order to inject into my writings that harsh note and black air that they no longer had when he ceased to direct me.'[94]

90. A. Pagden, *The Fall of Natural Man*, Cambridge, 1982, p. 9.
91. See H. Gouhier, '*Nature et histoire dans la pensée de J.-J. Rousseau*', *Annales*, XXXIII, pp. 7–48.
92. The *Supplément* was written between 1771 and 1773. (See G. Chinard's introduction to his edition, published Paris and Baltimore, 1935.) In his earlier writings Diderot had taken a more progressive view of human history.
93. *OC*, I, p. 389.
94. *OC*, I. p. 389 fn.

INTRODUCTION

When he first read the *Discourse on Inequality*, Diderot had nothing but praise for it, and since its argument was as close to his own philosophy as Rousseau was ever to be, one cannot doubt that Diderot's praise was sincere; and that he still looked on Rousseau as a friend, an ally in all his struggles to propagate the ideology of science.

Rousseau for his part still looked on Diderot as an ally in his particular struggles also. Having completed the *Second Discourse* during the winter of 1753–4, he left a copy of the text in Diderot's hands, hoping to have it published by Pissot in Paris.[95] He had no great expectations of winning the prize at Dijon, but he was eager to have the work brought as soon as possible to the attention of his readers and critics, since he believed it provided a systematic answer to the questions left unanswered in his first discourse, and to add, as it were, the authority of science to the eloquence of the moralist he had deployed in his previous writings.

Even so, he was not confident that his reasoning would be correctly understood, and he begged the public to read his text twice before coming to any conclusions about what he had to say. He knew himself to be in some ways the victim of his own paradoxes; he was also perhaps more than he realized the victim of his colourful literary style, of his gift for constructing an arresting and an unforgettable phrase. Many readers took his indictment of existing inequality among men in society to be a plea for universal equality, which is not at all what he had in mind. The kind of equality Rousseau desired was no more than that desired by Plato; he believed that everyone's place in society should correspond to everyone's merits or services. He was bitterly opposed to the situation he observed in France, where he saw the rich dominating the poor without being in any way morally better than the poor, but, on the contrary, worse.

Some readers took Rousseau's attacks on property to be a plea for communism, but, far from being a communist, he was only to a limited extent an egalitarian. He makes this abundantly clear in the last footnote to the *Second Discourse*:

> Distributive justice would still be opposed to the strict equality of the state of nature, even if it were practicable in civil society, and as all members of

95. In the event the *Discourse on Inequality* was published in Amsterdam by M.M. Rey, whose acquaintance Rousseau made in Geneva in 1754. Copies were on sale in May 1755 before Rousseau was able formally to present a copy to the authorities of Geneva.

the state owe it services proportionate to their talents and their strength, the citizens in turn ought to be honoured and favoured in proportion to their services.[96]

Justice did not require equality, but rather the placing of every man where he ought to be. But was there any community on earth where such a state of affairs existed? The answer that suggested itself to Rousseau was Geneva and hence it is not surprising that he should have decided to dedicate his *Discourse on Inequality* to that republic:

> Having had the good fortune to be born among you, [he wrote] how could I reflect upon the equality which nature established among men and the inequality which they have instituted among themselves without thinking of the profound wisdom with which the one and the other being happily combined in your Republic, contribute in the manner closest to natural law and most favourable to society, to the maintenance of public order and the wellbeing of individuals?

From words Rousseau passed to action, and he decided, at the age of forty-two, to visit once more the city from which he had run away as an unhappy apprentice twenty-six years before. This led him to seek to recover in Geneva the rights of a citizen he had lost when he converted to the Catholic Church in Turin at the age of sixteen. Such a recovery of his rights could not, however, be accomplished easily. In the first place, he would have to repudiate his obedience to Rome and, secondly, he would have to satisfy the authorities of the Calvinist Church of Geneva that he was now a sincere adherent of the Reformed religion. Could he do so?

One thing that seems certain is that Rousseau had kept his belief in God, and was distressed by the increasingly overt atheism of fellow Encyclopaedists and the salons. Mme d'Épinay, in her moral *L'Histoire de Mme de Montbrillant*, tells a story about her protagonist 'René' which is probably based on a true incident concerning Rousseau in 1754. At a *dîner d'adieu* to an actress friend who gives voice to atheist opinions, René (Rousseau) protests: 'if it is cowardice to tolerate anyone speaking ill of an absent friend, it is a crime to tolerate anyone speaking ill of God, who is present, and I, gentlemen, believe in God'; turning to the actress he says: 'the idea of God is necessary to happiness, and I want you to be happy'.[97] Rousseau made a somewhat similar scene

---

96. *OC*, III, pp. 222–3.   97. *J.-J.*, p. 316.

at Mme d'Holbach's salon, when Diderot, Saint-Lambert and other *philosophes* were tormenting a country priest who fancied himself as a dramatist.[98]

One cannot deny that Rousseau had some religious beliefs and some religious feelings.[99] But he claimed more. He claimed to be a Christian. He said that he read the Bible daily; that he believed in the existence of a merciful God and in the immortality of the soul. Would this be enough for Geneva? Or would it serve simply to alienate him from the atheists without reconciling him to the Calvinists?

He set off for Geneva on 1 June 1754, taking advantage of an offer of a lift in the carriage of a friend named Capperonnier de Gauffecourt, who had once been an opposition leader in Geneva but rallied to the government after the Mediation settlement of 1738 and secured as his reward a profitable salt monopoly. Rousseau, having implored the women of Geneva in the Dedication he wrote for his *Second Discourse* to exert their 'chaste power, solely within the marriage bond ... for the glory of the state', took with him his mistress, Thérèse Levasseur, and was only shocked that Gauffecourt tried to seduce her on the journey while his back was turned.

He arrived in Geneva determined to admire all he found: the people, the place, the institutions and the magistrates. He finished off the Dedication to his *Second Discourse* before he arrived, and signed it 'At Chambéry, 12 June, 1754'. His eulogism of Geneva was not empty hyperbole; and the reality he encountered seemed happily to confirm his expectations. In a letter he wrote on 12 July to Madame Dupin he said,

> I cannot tell you how much more beautiful Geneva seems to have become without anything having changed: the difference must be in my way of looking at it. What is certain is that Geneva appears as one of the most charming cities in the world, and its inhabitants the wisest and happiest men I know. Liberty is well established, the government is peaceful, the citizens are enlightened, solid and modest, knowing their rights and courageously upholding them and yet respecting those of others.[100]

Rousseau had told his friends in Paris that he was making the trip to Geneva only to secure official acceptance of the Dedication. In the

---

98. *J.-J.*, p. 313.
99. See P.M. Masson, *La Religion de J.-J. Rousseau*, 3 vols, Paris, 1916.
100. *CC*, III, pp. 16–18.

Confessions he says that he was so excited by the welcome he received in Geneva that he made up his mind to apply for the restoration of his rights as a citizen, a procedure that required his repudiation of Catholicism and re-admission to the Calvinist Church. 'I gave myself up to patriotic fervour and, ashamed of being excluded from my rights as a citizen because of my membership of a Church different from that of my forefathers, I decided openly to return to the Protestant Communion.'[101] This is not exactly the story told in Geneva at the time. It was said on his behalf that he came as a penitent and that he had already been preparing himself in Paris for his return to the Calvinist Church by attending services at the Dutch Ambassador's residence.

Whether this claim was true or false, Rousseau considered himself a sound enough believer in the Protestant form of the Christian religion to be admitted to the established Church, and although he was living in open union with a woman who was not his wife, he personally considered that his morals were irreproachable. He was given a friendly reception by the authorities and, doubtless because he was a celebrity, he was excused all the painful formalities of repentance required of ordinary applicants for re-admission to the Church; after a brisk interview by some broad-minded theologians – Latitudinarianism, if not actual unitarianism, having become fashionable in Geneva – he was restored to the role of communicant and citizen. His interlocutors seem to have averted their eyes from anything which might have disqualified him from re-admission. He spent a whole summer among friends in Geneva, rediscovering the beauties of alpine scenery.

But there could be no serious question of his settling permanently in Geneva, although he talked about doing so. There was not only the delicate question of Thérèse, and the gap which could not forever be veiled between his very minimal religion and the creed of the Calvinist Church; there was really no way for him to earn a living in Geneva. In a city without music he could not find work as a music copyist; and there were no rich patrons of philosophy and literature. Moreover, he soon learned that his proposed Dedication of the *Discourse on Inequality* to the Republic of Geneva caused only embarrassment. He was reminded that it was not correct for a Dedication

101. *OC*, I, p. 392.

to be addressed to the citizenry in general but that it should be addressed to the magistrates; and while there was no denying the gracious words about those magistrates in Rousseau's Dedication, they were very pointedly called 'Magnificent and Most Honourable Lords' whereas the citizens as a whole were addressed as 'Magnificent, Most Honourable and *Sovereign* Lords'. The whole exercise began to look tactless, or worse.

'You have depicted us as we ought to be, not as we are',[102] one of the Syndics of Geneva, Jean-Louis Du Pan, wrote to Rousseau after he had read the Dedication in print. At best Rousseau would seem to 'be teaching the Genevans a lesson'.[103] It was not unnatural that some readers should even suspect Rousseau of having intended all the time to attack the regime by the device of praising it where it least deserved praise and of showing how far it had fallen from its principles by expounding those principles which it had most conspicuously betrayed. But this, I believe, is to impute to Rousseau a more devious sophistication than he possessed as a polemicist. At the time he wrote the Dedication he still had his idealized conception of Geneva. It was what he saw there during the summer of 1754, his subsequent reflections and the painful experiences of 1762 – when his *Social Contract* and *Émile* were publicly burned in Geneva and a decree issued for the arrest of the author – that robbed Rousseau of his illusions about his native city.

After his summer in Geneva he returned for a time to the society of the *philosophes* in Paris. But he could no longer feel at home with them. Their success had made them more and more worldly, more and more a central part of that smart, rich world of Paris he had repudiated. As he meditated on his predicament there seemed to him only one option left, if there was no place for him in either Geneva or Paris, and that was to retire to the country. In time he was to become a sort of hermit, if admittedly a hermit under the protection of most exalted aristocrats, such as the Duc and Duchesse de Luxembourg, who provided him with a modest dwelling on their estate at Montmorency. Should we be surprised that the author of the *Discourse on Inequality* felt more at ease with members of the old *noblesse de race* in the Île de France than in the bourgeois salons of Paris? I do not think so.

102. *CC*, III, pp. 136–7.
103. Starobinski (*OC*, III, p. xlix).

INTRODUCTION

It was not simply a case of snobbery, but rather one of mature sympathy. Many French noblemen of ancient lineage despised as Rousseau did the alliance of riches and royal absolutism which dominated the kingdom. They could look back to France as it was before the Bourbon dynasty had introduced royal despotism and Richelieu had destroyed their fortified castles. They remembered feudal France, when a noble lord was master of his domains and owed only minimal obedience to the King. Of course, they had no actual memories of those days; but their historical imagination was based on well-established knowledge and accompanied by strong feelings of resentment towards the existing regime and of contempt both for those members of the aristocracy who had allowed themselves to be transformed into courtiers at Versailles and for the bourgeoisie who had bought up most of the wealth of the nation.

Their attitude to life was a form of romanticism. They knew their title to aristocracy was an empty one: it gave them privileges without power; they were superior in social rank, but abysmally inferior in political importance to the bureaucrats who served the King. The *noblesse de race* had their dreams of a France that was dead, when the ideals of chivalry had proclaimed that only men of noble character should lead and protect the people. Their dreams found an echo in Rousseau, with his dream of society where only those who served the nation best would be in superior positions. They knew that their world was dead, and Rousseau had come to realize that his ideal state, the perfectly balanced republic where men were free because they ruled themselves, was no longer alive in the modern world in the one place where it might have been. A pervasive melancholy infused all his future writings, despite their manly intellectual rigour and their vivid, exciting eloquence. Imagination suggested ways to happiness and freedom; experience showed that men could not be expected to follow them.

DISCOURSE ON THE ORIGINS AND FOUNDATIONS OF INEQUALITY AMONG MEN

by

Jean-Jacques Rousseau
CITIZEN OF GENEVA

It is not in depraved beings,
but in those who act in
accordance with nature that
we must seek what is natural.

    Aristotle, *Politics* (I.v.1254a)

To the Republic of Geneva
Magnificent, Most Honoured and Sovereign Lords

CONVINCED as I am that none but a virtuous citizen is entitled to render his country honours it can acknowledge, I have laboured for thirty years to earn the right to offer you public homage; and the present happy occasion making up in part for what my efforts alone would fail to achieve, I have come to believe that I might be allowed in this case to act upon the promptings of the zeal which inspires me rather than with the right which ought to be my authorization. Having had the good fortune to be born among you, how could I reflect upon the equality which nature established among men and the inequality which they have instituted among themselves, without thinking of the profound wisdom with which the one and the other, being happily combined in your Republic, contribute in the manner closest to natural law and most favourable to society to the maintenance of public order and the wellbeing of individuals? In searching for the best principles that good sense could dictate on the constitution of a government, I was so impressed at finding all of them put into practice in yours that even if I had not been born within your walls, I should have felt myself compelled to offer this picture of human society to that people which, among all others, seems to me to possess the greatest advantages of society and to have guarded most successfully against the abuses of society.

If I had had to choose the place of my birth, I would have chosen a society of which the dimensions were limited by the extent of human faculties, that is to say, by the possibility of being well governed; a society where everyone was equal to his job so that no one was obliged to commit to others the functions which belonged to him; a state where, every individual being acquainted with every other, neither the dark manoeuvres of vice nor the modesty of virtue was concealed from public gaze and judgement, a state where the delectable habit of meeting and knowing one another made love of country a love for fellow citizens rather a love for the land.

I would have wished to be born in a country where the sovereign and the people could have only a single and identical interest, so that all the movements of the civil machine always tended to promote the common happiness, and since this is something that cannot happen unless the sovereign and the people are one and the same person, it follows that I would have wished to be born under a wisely tempered democratic government.

I would have wished to live and die free, that is to say, subject to law in such a way that neither I nor anyone else could shake off the honourable yoke, that soft and salutary yoke which the proudest heads bear with all the more docility because they are made to bear none other.

I would have wished that no one within the state could claim to be above the law, and no one from outside could dictate any law that the state was bound to recognize. For whatever might be the formal constitution of a government, if there is one man who is not subject to the law, all the others will necessarily be at his discretion (A). And if there is one national ruler and another alien ruler, no matter what division of authority they could arrange between themselves, it is impossible for both to be duly obeyed or for the state to be well governed.

I would certainly not wish to live in a republic newly founded, however good its laws, for fear that the government might not fit the exigences of the moment, either not suiting the new citizens or the citizens not suiting the new government, so that the state would be liable to upheavals and destruction almost from its birth. For there is in freedom, as there is in heavy and succulent food or in rich wine, something which fortifies robust constitutions used to it, but which overwhelms, ruins and intoxicates weak and delicate people unused to it. Once a people is accustomed to masters, it is no longer in a condition to do without them. If such peoples try to shake off the yoke, they remove themselves even further from liberty; for as they mistake for liberty an unbridled licence which is the opposite of freedom, their revolutions almost always deliver them into the hands of seducers who multiply their chains. Even the Romans, that model of a free people, were in no situation to govern themselves when they first emerged from the oppression of the Tarquins. Debased by the slavery and ignominious toil that had been imposed upon them, they were at first only a stupid populace needing to be handled and governed with the utmost sagacity, so that in becoming accustomed little by little to breathing the salubrious air of freedom, souls which had been enervated, or rather brutalized, by tyranny, could acquire by degrees those austere morals and that noble courage which ultimately made them of all peoples the most worthy of respect. For this reason I would have sought as my own country a happy and peaceful commonwealth of which the history was lost, so to speak, in the darkness of time; one which had endured only such hostile attacks as might serve to bring forth and fortify the courage and patriotism of the inhabitants, a commonwealth whose citizens, being long accustomed to a wise independence, were not only free but fit to be free.

I would have wanted to choose as my country one delivered by a lucky incapacity from the fierce love of conquest and protected by an even more fortunate location from fear of becoming itself the object of conquest by any other state; a free city surrounded by several nations none of which had any interest in invading it, but all having an interest in preventing others from invading it, in a word, a republic which would not tempt the ambitions of its neighbours and might reasonably count on their support in case of need. It follows that a state in such a fortunate situation would have nothing to fear except from itself; and if its citizens were trained in arms, it would be for the sake of developing that soldierly ardour and noble courage which go so well with liberty and nourish men's taste for it rather than from the necessity of providing their defence.

I would have chosen a country where the right to legislate was common to all the citizens – for who could know better than they what laws would most suit their living together in the same society? But I would not have approved of plebiscites, like those of the Romans, whereby the rulers of the state and those most interested in its preservation were excluded from deliberations on which the safety of the state often depended and whereby the magistrates, by an absurd inconsistency, were deprived of rights which ordinary citizens enjoyed.

On the contrary, I would have desired, as a means of thwarting self-interested and ill-conceived projects and all such hazardous innovations as those which finally destroyed the Athenians, that no one should be at liberty to introduce new laws according to his fancy, but that the right of initiation should be vested uniquely in the magistrates, and that even they should invoke that right with so much circumspection, and the people, for their part, be so reluctant to give their consent to new laws, and new laws be promulgated with so much solemnity, that before the constitution could be disturbed, there would be time enough for everyone to reflect that it is above all the great antiquity of laws which makes them sacred and venerable, that men soon come to despise laws which can be changed every day; and that when the habit is acquired of neglecting ancient usages in the name of improvement, great evils are often introduced in the endeavour to correct lesser ones.

Above all, I would have fled from a republic, as one necessarily ill governed, where the people, believing themselves able either to do without magistrates altogether or to allow their magistrates only a very precarious authority, foolishly kept in their own hands the administration of civil affairs and the execution of their own laws. Such must have been the primitive constitution of the first governments which emerged immediately after the state of nature; it was also one of the vices which ruined the city-state of Athens.

I would have chosen a republic where the individuals, being content with sanctioning the laws and making decisions in assemblies on proposals from the leaders on the most important public business, had established courts, distinguishing carefully between the several parts of the constitution and elected year by year the most capable and the most upright of their fellow citizens to administer justice and govern the state; a republic where the virtue of the magistrates gave such manifest evidence of the wisdom of the people that each did the other a reciprocal honour. In such a case if ever some unhappy misunderstanding disturbed the civil harmony, even such intervals of blindness and error would be characterized by proofs of moderation, mutual esteem and universal respect for the laws – presages and guarantees of a sincere and permanent reconciliation.

Such, Magnificent, Most Honoured and Sovereign Lords, are the advantages I would have sought in the country I would have chosen as my own. And if Providence had added to all those merits a charming location, a temperate climate, a fertile countryside, and the most delectable appearance of any place under the sun, I would have wished to complete my fortune by enjoying all these advantages in the bosom of that happy country, living peacefully in sweet society with my fellow citizens, and, taking my example from them, exhibiting towards them humanity, friendship and all the virtues, and leaving after me the honourable memory of a good man and an upright, virtuous patriot.

If, less fortunate or wise too late, I were to find myself reduced to ending an infirm and languishing sojourn on earth in other climes, vainly regretting that repose and peace of which a misspent youth had robbed me, I would at least have kept alive in my soul the feelings that I was unable to express in my own country, and, prompted by a tender and disinterested love for my distant fellow citizens, I would have addressed to them from the bottom of my heart some such words as these:

My dear Fellow Citizens – or rather my Brothers – for ties of blood as well as the laws unite almost all of us – I am pleased to say that I cannot think of you without at the same time remembering all the blessings which you enjoy and of which none of you, perhaps, appreciates the value better than I, who have lost them. The more I reflect on your civil and political arrangements, the less can I imagine that the nature of human contrivance could produce anything better. Under all other governments, when it is a question of securing the greatest good of the state, everything is always limited to projects and ideas, at best to what is hypothetical. In your case, your happiness is already achieved; you have only to know how to be satisfied with it. Your sovereignty, acquired or recovered at the point of the sword and preserved throughout two centuries by the forces of valour and of wisdom, is at last fully and universally recognized.[1] Honourable treaties fix your frontiers, assure your rights, and secure your repose. Your constitution is excellent, dictated by the most exalted wisdom and guaranteed by friendly and estimable Powers; your state is tranquil; you have neither wars nor conquerors to fear; you have no masters other than wise laws instituted by yourselves and administered by upright magistrates of your own choosing; you are neither so rich as to be enervated by effeminacy and lose in vain luxury the taste for true felicity and solid virtue, nor are you so poor as to need from foreign aid more than your own industry can furnish; and, what is more, this precious liberty, which can be defended in great nations only by means of exorbitant taxation, costs you almost nothing to preserve.

Long may a republic so wisely and happily constituted endure, both for the felicity of its own citizens and as an example to other peoples! This is the only wish that remains for you to express and the only precaution that remains for you to undertake. It is for you alone henceforth, not to institute your happiness, for your ancestors have spared you that effort, but to make your happiness endure by the wisdom of using it well. Your preservation depends on your perpetual union, your obedience to the law and your respect for its ministers. If there remains among you one grain of bitterness or defiance, hasten to destroy it as a fatal leaven which must sooner or later generate misfortune for you and ruin for the state. I implore you all to look into the depths of your hearts and listen to the secret voice of conscience. Who among you knows in the whole universe a body of men more upright, more enlightened, more worthy of respect than your own magistrature? Do not all its members afford you an example of moderation, of simplicity in morals, of respect for the laws, and the most sincere spirit of reconciliation? Then place in those wise leaders without reserve that salutary confidence which reason owes to virtue; remember that they are of your own choosing, that they have justified your choice, and that the honours owed to those whom you have placed in positions of dignity necessarily reflect on yourselves. None of you is so little enlightened as to be unaware that when the force of the laws and the authority of their defenders is lost, there can be no security or liberty for anyone. What, then, remains for consideration among you except for you to do wholeheartedly and with a just confidence that which you would in any case be obliged to do by enlightened self-interest, duty and reason? Let never a culpable and fatal indifference towards the defence of the constitution make you neglect in case of need the wise advice of the most enlightened and zealous of your fellow-citizens, but let equity, moderation, and the most respectful firmness of purpose continue to regulate all your enterprises and display you to the whole world as a model of a valiant and modest people as jealous of its glory as of its freedom. Beware above all – and this will be my last piece of advice to you – of ever listening to sinister interpretations and malicious rumours, the secret motives of which are often more dangerous than the actions they report. A whole house wakes up and heeds the alarm at the first cry of a good and faithful watchdog who never barks except at the approach of thieves, but everyone detests the importunity of those noisy beasts who endlessly disturb the public peace and whose constant ill-timed warnings are ignored even at the moment when they may be needed.

And you, Magnificent and Most Honoured Lords, the worthy and revered Magistrates of a free people, allow me to offer you in particular my homage and my respect. If there is in the world a rank capable of conferring glory on those who occupy it, it is undoubtedly one acquired by talent and virtue, the rank of which you have proved yourselves worthy and to which your fellow citizens have raised you. Their merits add to yours a new lustre; and since you have been elected by men capable of governing others in order to govern themselves, I cannot but regard you as being placed as much above other magistrates as a free people – and particularly that free people you have the honour to lead – is placed above the populace of other states.

May I be allowed to cite an example of which better records ought to have been preserved and which will always live in my own heart? I cannot recall without the most tender emotions the memory of that virtuous citizen to whom I owe my birth, and who often spoke to me in childhood of the respect that is due to you. I see him still, living by the work of his hands, and nourishing his soul with the most sublime truths. I see Tacitus, Plutarch and Grotius bundled together in front of him with the tools of his trade. I see at his side a beloved son receiving with all too little profit the gentle instruction of the best of fathers. But if the follies of a misspent youth made me forget those wise lessons for a time, I have had the good fortune at last to realize that whatever propensity one may have towards vice, an education which has engaged the heart is unlikely to be lost for ever.

Such, Magnificent and Most Honoured Lords, are the citizens – and indeed even the common inhabitants – born in the state that you govern; such are those educated and sensible men, of whom such false and base ideas prevail in other countries, where they are spoken of as 'the workers' or 'the people'. My father, I am happy to admit, was in no way distinguished among his fellow citizens; he was as they all are, and yet he was such that there was no country where his acquaintance was not sought after, cultivated, and indeed cultivated with profit in the best society. It is not for me to speak – and thank heaven it is not necessary for anyone to speak – to you of the consideration which can rightly be expected from you by men of my father's quality, your equals by education and by rights of nature and birth, your inferiors by their own will and by the preference they owe – and accord – to your merit, a preference for which you in turn owe them a species of gratitude. I learn with keen satisfaction how much you temper in your dealings with them a gravity proper to ministers of the laws with gentleness and consideration, and how well you repay them in esteem and solicitude for what they owe you in obedience and respect, conduct so filled with justice and wisdom that it serves to remove further and further from living memory unfortunate events that need to be forgotten if they are never to be witnessed again;[2] conduct that is all the more visibly judicious insofar as this equitable and generous people does its duty as a pleasure and naturally loves to honour you, and those most ardent to uphold their own rights are most inclined to respect yours.

It ought not to be surprising that the leaders of a civil society should have its glory and happiness at heart, but it is a bonus for the repose of men when those who regard themselves as the Ministers, or rather the Masters of a holier and more sublime City, exhibit some love for the earthly city which has nourished them. How pleasing it is for me to be able to point to an exceedingly rare exception in our favour, and to number in the ranks of our best citizens those zealous custodians of the sacred articles of faith established by the laws, those venerable shepherds of souls, whose vigorous and engaging eloquence is all the more effective in transmitting the principles of the Gospel to men's hearts because they themselves begin by practising what they preach. Everyone knows with what success the great art of preaching is cultivated in Geneva. And yet, because people are all too accustomed to observing things said in one way and done in another, few realize to what extent the spirit of Christianity, the sanctity of morals, discipline towards oneself and gentleness towards others prevail in the body of our clergy. Perhaps it falls to the city of Geneva alone to offer the inspiring example of a perfect union between a society of theologians and men of letters. To a large extent it is their wisdom, their acknowledged moderation and their zeal for the prosperity of the state which provide the grounds of my hope for its perpetual tranquillity; and I note, astonishment and respect mixed with my pleasure, how much our clergy are horrified by the terrible precepts of those holy and barbarous men, of which history provides more than one example, who in order to uphold what they call the rights of God – that is to say, their own interests – have been all the less careful about human blood because they have flattered themselves that their own would always be spared.

Could I forget that precious half of the commonwealth which assures the happiness of the other, and whose sweetness and prudence maintain its peace and good morals? Lovable and virtuous women of Geneva – the destiny of your sex will always be to govern ours.[3] Happy are we so long as your chaste power, exerted solely within the marriage bond, makes itself felt only for the glory of the state and the wellbeing of the public! It was thus that the women commanded at Sparta, and thus that you deserve to command in Geneva. What barbarous man could resist the voice of honour and reason in the mouth of a gentle wife, and who not despise the vanity of luxury in contemplating your simple and modest dress which, deriving its lustre from the wearer, seems all the more becoming to beauty? It is for you, by your kindly and innocent dominion and by your subtle influence, to perpetuate love of the laws within the state and concord among citizens, to reunite in happy marriages families that are divided and, above all, to correct, through the persuasive sweetness of your lessons and the modest grace of your conversation, those excesses that our young people may pick up in other countries, from which, instead of all the useful things that might profit them, they bring back, together with the puerile manners and ridiculous airs that are acquired among loose women, an admiration for all kinds of so-called grandeur, those frivolous compensations for servitude which will never match the true value of a noble freedom. Continue, therefore, always to be as you are, chaste guardians of our morals and all the gentle bonds of our peace, exploiting on every occasion the rights of the heart and of nature in the interests of duty and virtue.

I flatter myself that I shall not be disproved by events in building my hopes for the common happiness of the citizens and the glory of the republic on such guarantees. I admit that with all these advantages, the republic will not shine with the brilliance that dazzles most eyes, and for which an immature and fatal taste is the most deadly enemy of happiness and freedom. Let a dissolute youth go elsewhere to seek easy pleasure and long repentance. Let those who set themselves up as men of taste admire in other places the magnificence of palaces, the beauty of carriages, splendid furnishings, the pomp of ceremonial and all the refinements of effeminacy and luxury. In Geneva, there will be only men; yet such a spectacle has its own undoubted value, and those who appreciate it will be worth more than those who admire all the rest.

Magnificent, Most Honoured and Sovereign Lords, deign to receive with the same goodness my respectful assurances of the interest I take in your common prosperity. If I have been so unlucky as to be guilty of some indiscreet verve in this lively effusion from the heart, I beg you to forgive what springs from the tender affection of a true patriot, and the ardent and legitimate zeal of a man who can imagine no greater felicity for himself than that of seeing you all happy.

> I am, with the deepest respect,
>   Magnificent, Most Honoured and Sovereign Lords,
>   Your very humble and very obedient servant
>   and fellow-citizen
>
>   Jean-Jacques Rousseau

Chambéry, June 12, 1754

PREFACE

THE most useful and the least developed of all the sciences seems to me to be that of man (B), and I venture to suggest that the inscription on the Temple of Delphi [Know Thyself] alone contains a precept which is more important and more challenging than all the heavy tomes of moralists. Hence I consider the subject of the present discourse to be one of the most interesting questions that philosophy can examine, and also, unfortunately for us, one of the thorniest for philosophers to resolve. For how can we know the source of inequality among men if we do not first have knowledge of men themselves? And how can man come to know himself as nature made him once he has undergone all the changes which the succession of time and things must have produced in his original constitution, and so distinguish that which belongs to his own essence from that which circumstances and progress have added to, or altered in, his primitive state? Like the statue of Glaucus, which time, the seas and the storms had so disfigured that it resembled less a god than a wild beast, the human soul modified in society by a thousand ever-recurring causes, by the acquisition of a mass of knowledge and errors, by mutations taking place in the constitution of the body, and by the constant impact of the passions, has changed in appearance to the point of becoming almost unrecognizable, and is no longer to be found; instead of a being acting always according to definite and invariable principles and possessed of that celestial and majestic simplicity which the Creator imprinted upon it, we discover only the false clash of passion believing itself to be reasoning and understanding inflamed to delirium.

What is even more cruel is that the whole progress of the human species removes man constantly farther and farther from his primitive state; the more we acquire new knowledge, the more we deprive ourselves of the means of acquiring the most important knowledge of all; and, in a sense, it is through studying man that we have rendered ourselves incapable of knowing him.

It is easy to see that we must examine the successive changes that have taken place in the human constitution if we are to find the first origin of the differences which distinguish men, who are, by common consent, as much equal by nature as were the animals of every species before diverse physical causes introduced the varieties we observe among them. In fact, it is inconceivable that those earliest changes, by whatever means they occurred, should have altered simultaneously and in the same manner all the individual members of a species; as it was, some came to be improved, some to deteriorate, through acquiring various characteristics, good or bad, which were not actually inherent in their nature, while others continued for a longer time in their original state. Such was the first source of inequality among men, and it is easier to explain it in these general terms than to determine the actual causes of it with precision.

Let my readers not imagine that I flatter myself as having seen what I believe to be so difficult to see. I have launched several arguments, I have hazarded several conjectures, less in the hope of resolving the question than with the intention of clarifying it and reducing it to its true form.[4] It will be easy for others to go further down the same path, without it being easy for anyone to reach the end. For it is no light enterprise to separate that which is original from that which is artificial in man's present nature, and attain a solid knowledge of a state which no longer exists, which perhaps never existed, and which will probably never exist, yet of which it is necessary to have sound ideas if we are to judge our present state satisfactorily. Indeed it would require more philosophy than people realize in anyone who undertook to determine exactly what precautions must be taken to ensure reliable observation in this field; and it would seem to me not beneath the dignity of the Aristotles and the Plinys of our time to provide a sound solution to the following problem: 'What experiments would be necessary to produce knowledge of natural man, and by what means could these experiments be conducted within society?' Far from undertaking to resolve this problem myself, I think I have meditated enough on the subject to venture to assert in advance that the greatest philosophers would not be too good to direct such experiments or the most powerful sovereigns to sponsor them – a collaboration it is hardly reasonable to expect, considering the perseverance, or rather the combination of enlightenment and goodwill, that would be needed from both parties to make it a success.

Such researches, so difficult to undertake, and so much neglected hitherto, are nevertheless the only means that remain to us of overcoming the mass of difficulties which deprives us of knowledge of the real foundations of human society. It is this ignorance of man's nature which creates such uncertainty and obscurity as to the correct definition of natural right; for the idea of right, says Monsieur Burlamaqui,[5] and even more the idea of natural right, is manifestly relative to the nature of man. Hence, M. Burlamaqui continues, it is from the very nature of man, of his constitution and his condition, that we must derive the principles of the science of natural law.

It is not without surprise, or without scandal, that one observes the small measure of agreement that prevails on this subject among the various authors who have dealt with it. Among the most weighty writers one hardly finds two who share the same opinion. Without speaking of the ancient philosophers, who seem to have made it their business to contradict one another on all the most fundamental principles, the Roman jurists put man and every other animal indifferently under the same natural law, because they considered as natural law, the rules nature imposes on itself instead of the rules it prescribes, or, rather, because of the particular sense in which those jurists understood the word 'law', they seem to have taken laws in this context only to mean the general regularities established by nature among animate beings for their own preservation. The Moderns, understanding by the word 'law' simply a rule prescribed to a moral being, that is, to an intelligent free being considered in its relation to other such beings, consequently limit the province of natural law to the one animal that is endowed with reason, man; but these authors, each defining natural law in his own way, have built on principles so metaphysical that there are very few people among us capable of understanding them, let alone of discovering them for themselves. In fact, all these scholarly men's definitions, otherwise in perpetual contradiction with each other, have one thing in common: that it is impossible to understand natural law and hence to obey it, without being a very great reasoner and a profound metaphysician. This, put precisely, means that men must have employed in establishing society an enlightened intelligence which is developed only with the greatest difficulty and among very few people within the bosom of society itself.

Since we have so little knowledge of nature and such imperfect agreement about the meaning of the word 'law', it would be very difficult to concur on a good definition of natural law.[6] All the definitions we find in books have besides the defect of lacking uniformity the further defect of being derived from several ideas which men do not have naturally, and the utility of which they cannot conceive until after they have emerged from the state of nature. Theorists begin by thinking out the rules which it would be opportune for men to establish among themselves for the common interest, and afterwards they give the name 'natural law' to the collection of those rules, with no proof of their authenticity other than the good that could be seen to result from the universal observance of them. This, assuredly, is a very easy way of compiling definitions and explaining the nature of things on the basis of a more or less arbitrary usefulness.

But so long as we have no knowledge of natural man, we shall wish in vain to ascertain the law which he has received from nature or that which best suits his constitution. All that we can clearly see on the subject of this law is that for it to be a law, not only must the will of the being it obliges be able to obey it consciously, but also, for it to be natural, it must be spoken directly by the voice of nature.

Leaving aside, then, all the scholarly books which teach us to see men only as men have made themselves, and reflecting instead on the first and simplest operations of the human soul, I believe I can discern two principles antecedent to reason: the first gives us an ardent interest in our own wellbeing and our own preservation, the second inspires in us a natural aversion to seeing any other sentient being perish or suffer, especially if it is one of our kind. It is from the concurrence and combination that our mind is able to make of these two principles – without there being any need to introduce the principle of sociability – that all the rules of natural law seem to me to flow; rules that reason is afterwards forced to re-establish on other foundations, when, as a result of successive developments, reason has succeeded in suffocating nature.[7]

In this way we are not obliged to make a man a philosopher before we can make him a man; his duties towards others will not be dictated by the belated lessons of wisdom, and so long as he does not resist the inner promptings of commiseration, he will never do harm to another man or indeed to any other sentient being, except in a legitimate case where his interest in his preservation is at stake, and he is obliged to give preference to himself. By these means, we can put an end to the age-old dispute as to whether natural law applies to animals, for while it is clear that animals, being devoid of intellect and free will, cannot recognize this law, yet by reason of the fact that they share, so to speak, in our nature by virtue of the sensitivity with which they are endowed, it follows that animals ought to have a share in natural right, and that men are bound by a certain form of duty towards them. It seems, in fact, that if I am obliged to refrain from doing any harm to my neighbour, it is less because he is a reasonable being than because he is a sentient one; and a quality which is common to beast and man ought to give the former the right not to be uselessly ill-treated by the latter.

This same study of original man, of his real needs, and of the fundamental principles of his duties, is moreover the only effective means of dispersing the host of difficulties which surrounds the problems of the origin of moral inequality, the true foundations of the body politic, the reciprocal rights of its members, and a thousand similar questions, as important as they are obscure.

Human society contemplated with a tranquil and disinterested eye appears at first to display only the violence of powerful men and the oppression of the weak; the mind is revolted by the harshness of the strong; one is impelled to deplore the blindness of the weak, and as nothing is less stable among men than these exterior relationships which are produced more often by chance than by thought, and since weakness or strength go by the names of poverty or riches, human institutions seem at first sight to be founded on piles of shifting sands. It is only by examining them more closely, and only after clearing away the sand and dust which surrounds the edifice that one sees the solid base on which it is built, and learns to respect its foundations. For without the serious study of man, of man's natural faculties and their successive developments, one will never succeed in analyzing these distinctions, and separating, within the present order of things, that which the divine will has contrived from that which human artifice claims as its own. The political and moral research arising from the important questions which I examine is therefore useful in every way, and the hypothetical history of governments is an instructive lesson for man in all respects. In considering what would have become of us if we had been abandoned to ourselves, we ought to learn to bless Him whose beneficent hand, correcting our institutions and giving them a solid base, has prevented those disorders which might have resulted from them, and given birth to our happiness by means which looked as if they must complete our misery.

> 'Learn what God has willed you to be
> And find your place in the human world'
> Persius, *Satires, III*, pp. 71–3.

Question
proposed by the Dijon Academy

'What is the origin of the inequality among men,
and is it authorized by natural law?'

NOTE ON THE FOOTNOTES

I HAVE added some footnotes* to this essay, following my lazy habit of working in fits and starts. These notes sometimes wander too far from the subject to be suitable for reading with the text. I have therefore placed them at the end; in the discourse itself I have done my best to keep to the direct path. Readers who have the courage to begin again may entertain themselves by tackling the byways and attempting to go through the footnotes; little harm will be done if others do not read them at all.

---

* Rousseau's footnotes are indicated by letters A–S and collected at the end of the *Discourse*, pp. 139–72. The translator's footnotes are indicated by figures.

DISCOURSE ON THE ORIGINS AND THE FOUNDATIONS OF INEQUALITY AMONG MEN

It is *of* man that I have to speak, and the question I am to examine tells me that I am going to speak *to* men, for such questions are not raised by those who are afraid of acknowledging truth. I shall therefore defend the cause of humanity with confidence before those men of wisdom who invite me to do so, and I shall not be dissatisfied with myself if I prove myself worthy of my subject and of my judges.

I discern two sorts of inequality in the human species: the first I call natural or physical because it is established by nature, and consists of differences in age, health, strength of the body and qualities of the mind or soul; the second we might call moral or political inequality because it derives from a sort of convention, and is established, or at least authorized, by the consent of men. This latter inequality consists of the different privileges which some enjoy to the prejudice of others – such as their being richer, more honoured, more powerful than others, and even getting themselves obeyed by others.

One cannot ask what is the source of natural inequality because the answer is proclaimed by the very definition of the word; still less can one inquire whether there is not some essential connection between the two types of inequality, for that would be asking in other words whether those who command are necessarily superior to those who obey, and whether bodily or intellectual strength, wisdom and virtue are always to be found in individuals in proportion to their power or wealth – a good question perhaps to be disputed among slaves in the hearing of their masters, but not at all suited to reasonable and free men in search of the truth.

What exactly is the object of this discourse? To pinpoint that moment in the progress of things when, with right succeeding violence, nature was subjected to the law; to explain by what sequence of prodigious events the strong could resolve to serve the weak, and the people to purchase imaginary repose at the price of real happiness.

The philosophers who have examined the foundations of society have all felt it necessary to go back to the state of nature, but none of them has succeeded in getting there. Some have not hesitated to attribute to men in that state of nature the concept of just and unjust, without bothering to show that they must have had such a concept, or even that it would be useful to them. Others have spoken of the natural right each has to keep and defend what he owns without saying what they mean by 'own'. Others again, starting out by giving the stronger authority over the weaker, promptly introduce government, without thinking of the time that must have elapsed before the words 'authority' and 'government' could have had any meaning among men. Finally, all these philosophers talking ceaselessly of need, greed, oppression, desire and pride have transported into the state of nature concepts formed in society. They speak of savage man and they depict civilized man. It has not even entered the heads of most of our philosophers to doubt that the state of nature once existed, yet it is evident from reading the Scriptures that the first man, having received the light of reason and precepts at once from God, was not himself in the state of nature; and giving the writings of Moses that credence which every Christian philosopher owes them, one must deny that even before the Flood men were in the pure state of nature, unless they relapsed into it through some extraordinary event – a paradox that would be troublesome to uphold and altogether impossible to prove.

Let us begin by setting aside all the facts,[8] because they do not affect the question. One must not take the kind of research which we enter into as the pursuit of truths of history, but solely as hypothetical and conditional reasonings, better fitted to clarify the nature of things than to expose their actual origin; reasonings similar to those used every day by our physicists to explain the formation of the earth. Religion commands us to believe that since God himself withdrew men from the state of nature they are unequal because he willed that they be; but it does not forbid us to make conjectures, based solely on the nature of man and the beings that surround him, as to what the human race might have become if it had been abandoned to itself. This is what is asked of me and what I propose to examine in this discourse. Since my subject concerns men in general, I shall try to use terms intelligible to all peoples, or rather, forgetting time and place in order to think only of the men to whom I speak, I shall imagine myself in the Lyceum of Athens, repeating the lessons of my masters, having a Plato and a Xenocrates for my judges, and the human race for my audience.

O Man, to whatever country you belong and whatever your opinions, listen: here is your history as I believe I have read it, not in the books of your fellow men who are liars but in Nature which never lies. Everything which comes from her will be true; there will be nothing false except that which I have intermixed, unintentionally, of my own. The times of which I am going to speak are very remote – how much you have changed from what you were! It is, so to say, the life of your species that I am going to describe, in the light of the qualities which you once received and which your culture and your habits have been able to corrupt but not able to destroy. There is, I feel, an age at which the individual would like to stand still; you are going to search for the age at which you would wish your whole species had stood still. Discontented with your present condition for reasons which presage for your unfortunate posterity even greater discontent, you will wish perhaps you could go backwards in time – and this feeling must utter the eulogy of your first ancestors, the indictment of your contemporaries, and the terror of those who have the misfortune to live after you.

PART ONE

HOWEVER important it may be in order to reach a true judgement of man's natural state, to look back to his origins and examine him, so to speak, in the first embryo of his species, I do not propose to follow his organic system through all its successive developments. I shall not pause to investigate in the animal system what man must have been at the beginning in order to become in the end what he is. I shall not ask whether man's elongated nails were not originally, as Aristotle thought, hooked claws, whether his body was not covered with hair like a bear, or whether walking on all fours (C), with his eyes directed towards the earth and his vision confined to several paces, did not shape the character and the limits of his ideas.[1] On this subject I could offer only vague and almost wholly imaginary conjectures. Comparative anatomy has as yet made too little progress, the observations of naturalists are still too uncertain to furnish the basis of solid reasoning. Thus, without having recourse to the supernatural knowledge we possess on this subject and without regard to the changes that must have taken place in man's configuration, both inwardly and outwardly, as he put his limbs to new uses and nourished himself on new kinds of food, I shall suppose him to have been at all times as I see him today, walking on two feet, using his hands as we use ours, casting his gaze over the whole of nature and measuring with his eyes the vast expanse of the heavens.

If I strip the being thus constituted of all the supernatural gifts that he may have received, and of all the artificial faculties that he can have acquired only through a long process of time, if I consider him, in a word, as he must have emerged from the hands of nature, I see an animal less strong than some, less agile than others, but taken as a whole the most advantageously organized of all. I see him satisfying his hunger under an oak, quenching his thirst at the first stream, finding his bed under the same tree which provided his meal; and, behold, his needs are furnished.

The earth, left to its natural fertility (D) and covered with immense forests that no axe had ever mutilated, would afford on all sides storehouses and places of shelter to every species of animal. Man, dispersed among the beasts, would observe and imitate their activities and so assimilate their instincts, with this added advantage that while every other species has only its own instinct, man, having perhaps none which is peculiar to himself, appropriates every instinct, and by nourishing himself equally well on most of the various foods (E) the other animals divide among themselves, he finds his sustenance more easily than do any of the others.

Accustomed from infancy to the inclemencies of the weather and the rigours of the seasons, used to fatigue and forced to defend themselves and their prey naked and unarmed against other wild beasts or to escape from them by running faster than they, men develop a robust and almost immutable constitution. Children, coming into the world with the excellent physique of their fathers, and strengthening it by the same exercises which produced it, thus acquire all the vigour of which the human race is capable. Nature treats them exactly as the Law of Sparta treated the children of its citizens: it makes those who are well constituted strong and robust and makes the others die, thus differing from our own societies, where the state, by making children a burden to their fathers, kills them indiscriminately[2] before they are born.

The body of a savage being the only instrument he knows, he puts it to all sorts of uses of which our bodies, for lack of practice, are incapable; our equipment deprives us of that strength and agility which necessity obliges him to acquire. If he had had an axe, would his wrist have been able to break such solid branches? If he had had a sling, would his hand have been able to throw a stone with such speed? If he had had a ladder, would he have been able to climb a tree so nimbly? If he had had a horse, would he have been able to run so fast? Let the civilized man gather all his machines around him, and no doubt he will easily beat the savage; but if you would like to see an even more unequal match, pit the two together naked and unarmed, and you will soon see the advantages of having all one's forces constantly at one's command, of being always prepared for any eventuality, and of always being, so to speak, altogether complete in oneself (F).

Hobbes[3] claims that man is naturally intrepid and seeks only to attack and fight. An illustrious philosopher thinks, on the contrary, and Cumberland[4] and Pufendorf[5] also assert, that there is nothing so timid as man in the state of nature, that he is always trembling and ready to run away at the least noise he hears or the smallest movement he observes. This may well be true of things he does not know, and I do not doubt that he is frightened by any fresh scene when he cannot measure the physical good or evil to be expected, or compare his strength to the dangers he is to meet. Yet such circumstances are rare in the state of nature, where all things proceed in a uniform manner, and where the face of the earth is not subject to those abrupt and constant changes which are caused by the passions and caprices of civilized communities. The savage, living among the animals and placed from an early stage where he has to measure himself against them, soon makes the comparison, and perceiving that he excels the beasts in skill more than they surpass him in strength, learns to fear them no longer. Pit a bear or a wolf against a savage – robust, agile and courageous as all savages are – arm him with stones and a good stick, and you will find that the danger will be at least mutual; and that after a few such experiences, wild beasts, which do not like to attack their own kind, will not be eager to attack man either, having found him to be altogether as ferocious as they are themselves. In the case of animals that really do have more strength than he has skill, man is in the same situation as other weaker species, which nevertheless subsist, except indeed that he has the advantage that, being no less swift than they in running, and finding an almost certain refuge in any tree, he can either accept or refuse an encounter; he has the choice between flight and combat. Let us note also that it seems that no animal naturally makes war on man except in a case of self-defence or from extreme hunger, nor does an animal exhibit towards man any of those violent antipathies which seem to be the mark of a species destined by nature to serve as the food of another.* Man has other enemies, which are much more intimidating and against which he has not the same means of defending himself; his natural infirmities – infancy old age, and illnesses of every kind – melancholy proofs of our own weakness, the first two

---

*This no doubt explains why Negroes and savages are scarcely disturbed by the wild beasts they meet in the woods. The Caribs of Venezuela among others live in this way, in the most perfect security and without the least trouble. Even though they are almost naked, says François Coréal,[6] they do not hesitate to expose themselves in the woods armed solely with bows and arrows; yet we never hear of any one of them being devoured by wild beasts [Edition of 1782].

being common to all animals, the last belonging chiefly to man as he lives in society. Indeed on the subject of infancy, I notice that the human mother, carrying her child with her everywhere, can feed it with greater ease than can the females of many other animals, which are forced to move to and fro constantly and with much fatigue, going in one direction to find food and in the other to suckle or nourish their young. It is true that if the human mother happens to perish, her child is in great danger of perishing with her; but this hazard is common to a hundred other species, of which the young are unable for a considerable time to find their own food. And if infancy lasts longer among us (G), our lives are longer, too; so that all things are more or less equal in this respect, even though there are other factors governing the duration of childhood and the number of young (H) which are not relevant to the present subject. In the case of old people, who are less active and sweat little, the need for food diminishes with the ability to acquire it – and since the life of the savage spares him from gout and rheumatism, and since old age is of all ills the one that human aid is least able to relieve, savages die in the end without others noticing that they have ceased to exist and almost without noticing it themselves.

On the question of sickness I shall not repeat the vain and empty declamations against medicine that are uttered by most people when they are healthy, but I will ask whether there is any solid evidence for concluding that in the country where medicine is most rudimentary the average life of men is shorter than it is in the country where that art is cultivated with the greatest care; and how indeed could that be the case if we bring upon ourselves more diseases than medicine can furnish remedies? The extreme inequality of our ways of life, the excess of idleness among some and the excess of toil among others, the ease of stimulating and gratifying our appetites and our senses, the over-elaborate foods of the rich, which inflame and overwhelm them with indigestion, the bad food of the poor, which they often go without altogether, so that they over-eat greedily when they have the opportunity; those late nights, excesses of all kinds, immoderate transports of every passion, fatigue, exhaustion of mind, the innumerable sorrows and anxieties that people in all classes suffer, and by which the human soul is constantly tormented:[7] these are the fatal proofs that most of our ills are of our own making, and that we might have avoided nearly all of them if only we had adhered to the simple, unchanging and solitary way of life that nature ordained for us. If nature destined us to be healthy, I would almost venture to assert that the state of reflection is a state contrary to nature, and that the man who meditates is a depraved animal. When we think of the good constitution of savages — at least of those we have not corrupted with our strong liquors — and reflect that they have almost no disorders except wounds and old age, we are almost prompted to believe that we could write the history of human illness by following the history of civilized societies. Such at least was the opinion of Plato, who deduced from the fact that certain remedies were used or approved by Podalirius and Machaon at the siege of Troy, that the various sicknesses which could be provoked by these remedies, were not then known to mankind.*

With so few sources of illness, man in the state of nature has little need for remedies, and even less for physicians; the human race is, in this respect, in no worse a condition than any other species; and we can easily learn from hunters whether they find sick animals in the field. Assuredly, they find many which have received serious wounds that have healed very well, which have had bones or even limbs broken and restored by no other surgeon than time and by no other regimen than their ordinary life, without being any the less perfectly healed, as a result of not having been tormented with incisions, poisoned with drugs or wasted by fasting. In short, however useful medicine well administered may be for us, it is certain that if a sick savage abandoned to himself has nothing to hope for except from nature, conversely he has nothing to fear except from his sickness, all of which makes his situation very often preferable to our own.

Let us therefore beware of confusing savage man with the man we have before our eyes. Nature treats every animal abandoned to her care with a partiality which seems to prove how jealous she is of that right. The horse, the cat, the bull and even the ass are for the most part larger and all have a more robust constitution, more vigour, more strength and more spirit in the forest than under our roofs; they lose half those advantages on becoming domesticated, and

* Paracelsus reports that dieting, so necessary today, was first invented by Hippocrates (See Plato's *Republic*, *III*, 405d and Homer's *Iliad*, *XI*, 639).

one might say that all our efforts to care for and feed these animals have only succeeded in making them degenerate. The same is true even of man himself; in becoming sociable and a slave, he grows feeble, timid, servile; and his soft and effeminate way of life completes the enervation both of his strength and his courage. Furthermore, the difference between savage and the domesticated man must be greater than the difference between wild and tame animals, for since men and beasts are treated equally by nature, all the commodities which man gives himself beyond those he gives to the animals he tames, are so many particular factors that make him degenerate more appreciably.

Being naked, homeless and deprived of all those useless things we believe so necessary is no great misfortune for these first men, and above all no great obstacle to their preservation. If their skins are not covered with hair, they have no need of it in warm countries and in cold countries they soon learn to put on the skins of the beasts they have vanquished. If they have only two legs for running, they have two arms with which to defend themselves and to provide their needs; their children learn to walk tardily perhaps and with difficulty, but their mothers can carry them with ease, an advantage lacked by other species, where the mother, if she is pursued, finds herself forced either to abandon her young or to move at their pace.* Finally, unless we postulate a certain singular and fortuitous concurrence of circumstances of which I shall speak later, and which could very well never happen, it is clear that the first man who made himself clothing and a lodging provided himself with things that were not really necessary, since he had done without up to that time; and it is hard to see why he could not endure as a grown man the kind of life he had endured from his infancy.

Solitary, idle, and always close to danger, the savage cannot but enjoy sleeping; and he must sleep lightly like the animals, which think little and may be said to sleep all the time they are not thinking. Self preservation being the savage's only concern, his best

---

* There may be some exceptions to this: for example, the animal in the province of Nicaragua which resembles a fox, and has feet like the hands of a man and which, according to Coréal,[8] has under its stomach a pouch where the mother puts her young whenever she is obliged to flee. This is doubtless the same animal which is called in Mexico *tlaquatzin*, the female of which is said by Laët[9] to have a similar pouch for the same purpose.

trained faculties must be those which have as their main object attack and defence – either to subdue a prey or to avoid becoming the prey of another animal. On the other hand, those organs which are developed only by softness and sensuality must remain in a rudimentary state, precluding any kind of delicacy; and his five senses will be found to be distributed in this way: he will have touch and taste in an extremely coarse form, but sight, hearing and smell in a most subtle form; and what is true of animals in general is also, according to the reports of explorers, true of most savage peoples. Hence we must not be astonished that the Hottentots[10] of the Cape of Good Hope see ships on the high seas with the naked eye from the same distance that the Dutch see with their telescopes, or that the American savages[11] scent Spaniards on the trail as well as do the best dogs; or that all these barbarous nations endure their nakedness without discomfort or that they sharpen their palates with peppers and drink strong European liquors like water.

I have so far considered only the physical man; let us try to look at him now in his metaphysical and moral aspects.

I see in all animals only an ingenious machine to which nature has given senses in order to keep itself in motion and protect itself, up to a certain point, against everything that is likely to destroy or disturb it. I see exactly the same things in the human machine, with this difference: that while nature alone activates everything in the operations of a beast, man participates in his own actions in his capacity as a free agent. The beast chooses or rejects by instinct, man by an act of freewill, which means that the beast cannot deviate from the laws which are prescribed to it, even when it might be advantageous for it to do so, whereas a man often deviates from such rules to his own prejudice. That is why a pigeon would die of hunger beside a dish filled with choice meats and a cat beside a pile of fruits or grain, even though either could very well nourish itself with the foods it disdains, if only it were informed by nature to try them. Then we see, too, that dissolute men abandon themselves to the excesses that bring on fevers and death, because the intellect depraves the senses and the will continues to speak when nature is silent.

Every animal has ideas because it has senses; up to a certain point it even associates those ideas; and man differs from the beasts in this respect only in a matter of degree. Some philosophers have even asserted that there is more difference between one given man and another than there is between a given man and a given beast. Thus it is not his understanding which constitutes the specific distinction of man among all other animals, but his capacity as a free agent. Nature commands all animals, and the beast obeys. Man receives the same impulsion, but he recognizes himself as being free to acquiesce or resist; and it is above all in this consciousness of his freedom that the spirituality of his soul reveals itself,[12] for physics explains in a certain way the mechanism of the senses and the formation of ideas, but in the power to will, or rather to choose, and in the feeling of that power, we see pure spiritual activity, of which the laws of mechanics can explain nothing.

But while the difficulties which surround all these questions may allow some room for disagreement about this difference between man and beast, there is one further distinguishing characteristic of man which is very specific indeed and about which there can be no dispute, and that is *the faculty of self-improvement* – a faculty which, with the help of circumstance, progressively develops all our other faculties, and which in man is inherent in the species as much as in the individual. On the other hand an animal at the end of several months is already what it will remain for the rest of its life and its species will still be at the end of a thousand years what it was in the first of those thousand years. Why is man alone liable to grow into a dotard? Is it not the case that in doing so he returns to his primitive state, and that whereas the beast, which has acquired nothing and has correspondingly nothing to lose, always retains its instincts, man, losing through old age or through some accident, everything that the *faculty of self-improvement*[13] has enabled him to acquire, falls lower even than the beast? It would be sad for us to be forced to admit that this distinguishing and almost unlimited faculty of man is the source of all his misfortunes; that it is this faculty which, by the action of time, drags man out of that original condition in which he would pass peaceful and innocent days; that it is this faculty, which, bringing to fruition over the centuries his insights and his errors, his vices and his virtues, makes man in the end a tyrant over himself and over nature (I). It would be a terrible thing to be obliged to praise as a benefactor he who first suggested to the inhabitants of the shores of the Orinoco the practice of flattening the foreheads of their infants, and so preserving at least a part both of their imbecility and of their original happiness.[14]

The savage man, consigned by nature to instinct alone – or rather compensated for any lack of instinct by faculties capable of supplementing it at first and afterwards of lifting him far above it – begins with purely animal functions (J); perceiving and feeling will be his first experience in common with that of every other animal. Willing and rejecting, desiring and fearing will be the first and almost the only operations of his soul until such time as new circumstances cause new developments within it.

Whatever our moralists say, human understanding owes much to the passions, which, by common consent, also owe much to it. It is by the activity of the passions that our reason improves itself; we seek to know only because we desire to enjoy; and it is impossible to conceive a man who had neither desires nor fears giving himself the trouble of reasoning. The passions, in turn, owe their origin to our needs and their development to our knowledge, for one can desire or fear a thing only if one has an idea of it in the mind – unless one is responding to a simple impulsion of nature. The savage man, deprived of any sort of enlightenment, experiences passions only of this last kind; his desires do not go beyond his physical needs (K); the only good things he knows in the universe are food, a female and repose, and the only evils he fears are pain and hunger. I say pain and not death, because an animal will never know what death is, knowledge of death and its terrors being one of the first acquisitions which man gains on leaving the animal condition.

It would be easy for me, if it were necessary, to support this belief with facts, and to show how among all the nations of the world the progress of mind is exactly proportionate to the needs which those people have received from nature, or which circumstances have imposed on them, and is therefore proportionate to the passions which have prompted them to satisfy their needs. I would show how the arts were born in Egypt, and spread with the flooding waters of the Nile; I would follow their progress into Greece, where they took fresh root and grew and lifted themselves to the heavens from among the sands and rocks of Attica, without being able to germinate on the fertile banks of the Eurotas. I would observe that in general the peoples of the North are more industrious than those of the South, because they can less afford not to be; it is as if nature had chosen to equalize things by giving to men's minds the fertility it denied to the soil.[15]

But without recourse to the uncertain testimony of history, who does not see that everything appears to remove the savage man both from the temptation to quit the savage condition and from the means of doing so? His imagination paints no pictures; his heart yearns for nothing; his modest needs are readily supplied at hand; and he is so far from having enough knowledge for him to desire to acquire more knowledge, that he can have neither foresight nor curiosity. The prospect of the natural world leaves him indifferent just because it has become familiar. It is always the same pattern, always the same rotation. He has not the intelligence to wonder at the greatest marvels; and we should look in vain to him for that philosophy which a man needs if he is to know how to notice once what he has seen every day. His soul, which nothing disturbs, dwells only in the sensation of its present existence, without any idea of the future, however close that might be, and his projects, as limited as his horizons, hardly extend to the end of the day. Such is, even today, the extent of the foresight of a Caribbean Indian: he sells his cotton bed in the morning, and in the evening comes weeping to buy it back, having failed to foresee that he would need it for the next night.

The more we reflect on this subject, the more the distance between pure sensation and the simplest knowledge enlarges before our eyes, and it is impossible to conceive how any man acting by his own faculties alone, and without the help of communication or the stimulus of necessity, could bridge so great a gulf. How many centuries must have elapsed before men reached the point of seeing any other fire than that in the sky? How many computations of chance were needed to teach them the simplest uses of that element? How many times did they let their fires go out without knowing how to rekindle them? And how many times did the knowledge of such secrets die with the men who discovered them? What are we to say about agriculture, that art which requires so much industry and so much forethought, which depends on so many other arts, and which obviously is practicable only where society has at least started to exist; an art that we use not so much to make the earth yield foodstuffs, which she could do without help, but rather to force her to satisfy those preferences which are most to our taste. But suppose that men became so numerous that natural produce could no longer suffice to feed them – a supposition that, we may remark in passing, would demonstrate a great advantage for the human species in that way of life – suppose that, without forges or workshops, the tools of farming had fallen from heaven into the hands of savage men, and that they had overcome the mortal hatred that all men have for continuous labour; suppose that they had learned to foresee their needs very far in advance, that they had guessed how to cultivate the soil, sow seeds and plant trees; suppose that they had discovered the art of grinding wheat and fermenting the grape – all things they would have had to be taught by the Gods, for one cannot conceive how they could have learned them on their own:[16] after all this, what man would be foolish enough to break his back cultivating a field that would be stripped bare by the first comer – man or beast – to appreciate his harvest! And can any man resolve to devote his life to painful toil when the more he needs the produce of that toil the more sure he is to lose it? In a word, how can scarcity drive men to cultivate the land unless the land is divided among them: that is to say, until the state of nature has been abolished?

Even if we wanted to suppose savage man as skilled in the art of thinking as our philosophers depict him; if, following their example, we made him a philosopher, as well, discovering alone the most sublime truths and, by a process of the most abstract reasoning, formulating for himself maxims of justice and reason derived from the love of order or the known will of his Creator; in a word, if we assumed his mind to have all the intelligence and enlightenment it needs to have, and then found it to be in fact dull and stupid, what would be the use of all this metaphysics to a species who could not communicate and which would perish with the man who invented it? What progress could the human race make, scattered among the animals in the woods? And to what extent could men improve themselves and acquire knowledge by mutual endeavour when, having neither fixed abodes nor the least need for one another, they would perhaps hardly meet twice in their lives, without recognizing or speaking to one another?

Let it be remembered how many ideas we owe to the use of language; how much grammar exercises and facilitates the operations of the mind. Think of the unbelievable efforts and the infinite time that the first invention of language must have cost. Put these reflections together, and one can appreciate how many thousands of centuries must have been required for the progressive development within the human mind of all the operations of which it is capable.

Let me be allowed to consider for a moment the difficulties concerning the origin of language.[17] I might content myself by citing or reproducing here the researches that the Abbé de Condillac[18] has published on this problem, all of which abundantly confirm my own thoughts and which perhaps indeed gave me the original idea of them. But the way in which that philosopher resolves the difficulties he makes for himself on the origin of words shows that he assumes what I call into question, namely, some sort of society already established among the inventors of language; so I think that in referring to his ideas I ought to add my own, in order to explain the same difficulties in terms suited to my argument. The first difficulty we meet is that of imagining how language could have become necessary, for since men had no communication with each other nor any need for it, one cannot conceive the necessity of language or its possibility, were it not indispensable. I might assert, with many others, that languages were born in the domestic relationships of fathers, mothers and children; but that would not only fail to answer any objection, it would be to repeat the mistake of those who explain the state of nature with ideas derived from civil society, imagining the family already united under a single roof, its members cherishing among themselves a union as intimate and permanent as those which exist in our world, where numerous common interests bind families together, whereas among peoples in the primitive condition, having neither houses nor huts,[19] nor any kind of property, everyone slept where he chanced to find himself, and often for one night only; as males and females united fortuitously according to encounters, opportunities and desires, they required no speech to express the things they had to say to each other, and they separated with the same ease (L). The mother nursed her children at first to satisfy her own needs, then when habit had made them dear to her, she fed them to satisfy their needs; as soon as they had the strength to find their own food, they did not hesitate to leave their mother herself; and as there was virtually no way of finding one another again once they had lost sight of each other, they were soon at the stage of not even recognizing one another. Notice again that it is the child who has all his needs to express, and hence has more things to say to his mother than she has to say to him; from which it follows that the child must take the greatest part in inventing language, and the language he uses must be for the most part his own production – all of which multiplies languages by as many times as there are individuals to speak them. This is further compounded by a wandering, vagabond life which would leave no time for any language to acquire stability: for to say that the mother teaches the child the words he must use to express his desire for this or that object is to explain well enough the teaching of languages already formed, but it does not explain how languages are formed in the first place.

Let us suppose that first difficulty overcome; let us leap for a moment across that immense divide that separates the pure state of nature from the need for language, and let us inquire – assuming them to be necessary (M) – how languages could begin to be established. Here we meet a fresh difficulty, even worse than the previous one, for if men needed speech in order to learn to think, they needed still more to know how to think in order to discover the art of speech. And even if we could understand how the sounds of the voice came to be taken as the conventional interpreters of our ideas, it would still remain to be explained who could have been the conventional interpreters of this convention for ideas that have no perceptible object and could not therefore be indicated either by gesture or by the voice. Hence we can hardly formulate any defensible hypothesis about the birth of this art of communicating our thoughts and establishing intercourse between minds – this sublime art which, remote as it is from its origin, the philosopher still sees at such a prodigious distance from its perfection, that there can be no man rash enough to guarantee that it will ever arrive there, even if the revolutions that time necessarily brings were suspended in its favour, and prejudices to disappear from the academies, or be silent within them, and those academies could dedicate themselves for centuries without interruption to this thorny problem.

Man's first language, the most universal and energetic language, and the only one he needed before it was necessary to make persuasive speeches to assemblies of men, is the cry of nature. As this cry was uttered by a sort of instinct in times of pressing urgency, to beg for help in great danger or for relief in intense suffering, it was not much use in the course of ordinary life, where more moderate feelings prevailed. When the thoughts of men began to extend and to multiply, and more intimate communication was established among them, they looked for a greater number of signs and a more extensive language. They multiplied the inflections of the voice, and combined them with gestures, which are by nature more expressive, and which depend less for their meaning on any prior agreement. Thus visible and movable objects were expressed by gesture, and audible ones by imitative sounds; but since gestures can serve only to indicate objects which are actually present or are easily described and actions which are visible, and since gestures are not universally effective, being rendered useless by darkness or the interposition of a screening body, and require people's attention rather than excite it, man must eventually have thought of using instead articulations of the voice, which, without having the same direct relationship with certain ideas, are better suited to represent ideas as words or conventional signs. Such a substitution of voice for gesture can only have been made by a common consent, something rather difficult to put into effect by men whose crude organs had not yet been exercised; something indeed, even more difficult to conceive as happening in the first place, for such a unanimous agreement would need to be proposed, which means that speech seems to have been absolutely necessary to establish the use of speech.

One must conclude that the first words men used had a much wider signification in their minds than do words employed in languages already formed; and that as men had no knowledge of the division of language into the parts of speech, they gave each word the meaning of a whole proposition. When men began to distinguish subject from attribute, and verbs from nouns, which was itself no mediocre effort of genius, substantives were at first only so many proper nouns, the infinitive* was the sole tense of verbs, and so far as adjectives are concerned the very notion of them must have developed with great difficulty, since every adjective is an abstract word, and abstract thinking is a painful and not very natural process.

Each object was given at first a particular name, without regard to genus and species, which those first founders of language were

---

* The present infinitive [Edition of 1782].

incapable of distinguishing; and each individual thing presented itself in isolation to men's minds as it did in the panorama of nature. If one oak was called A and another oak was called B*,[20] it follows that the more limited the knowledge the more extensive the dictionary. The troublesomeness of all this nomenclature could not easily be relieved, for in order to arrange things under common and generic denominators, one must know their properties and the differences between them; one must have observations and definitions; that is to say, one must have more natural history and metaphysics than men of those times could possibly have had.

What is more, general ideas can only be introduced into the mind with the assistance of words; and the understanding can grasp them only by means of propositions. This is one of the reasons why animals cannot formulate such ideas and can never acquire that capacity for self-improvement which depends on them. When a monkey passes without hesitation from one nut to another, do you think he has a general idea of the type of fruit it is, or that he compares the two particular nuts with their archetype? Assuredly not; the sight of one of the nuts recalls to his memory the sensation he received from the other, and his eyes, modified in a certain manner, signal to his sense of taste the modification it is about to receive. All general ideas are purely intellectual; if the imagination intervenes to the least degree, the idea immediately becomes particular. Try to draw in your mind the picture of a tree in general and you will never succeed; despite yourself, a tree must be seen as small or large, sparse or leafy, light or dark, and if it resulted in your seeing only what is found in every tree, that image would no longer resemble a tree. Purely abstract entities are seen in the same way, or are conceivable only by means of words. Only the definition of a triangle gives you a true idea of it, and as soon as you imagine one in your mind, it becomes one particular triangle, and not another; and you cannot avoid making its lines perceptible or its plane coloured. It is therefore necessary to state a proposition, necessary to speak in order to have general ideas; for as soon as the imagination stops, the mind moves forward only with the aid of language. Hence, if the first inventors of speech could give

* For the first idea one derives from observing two things is that they are not the same, and it often requires a great deal of time to discern what they have in common [Edition of 1782].

names only to ideas they already possessed, it follows that the first substantives can never have been other than proper nouns.

But when our new grammarians began – by what means I cannot conceive – to enlarge their ideas and to generalize their words, the ignorance of the inventors must have subjected this method to very narrow limitations; and just as they must at first have produced too great a multiplicity of nouns of individuals for lack of knowledge of genera and species, they must afterwards have produced too few genera and species for want of discriminating between the differences in things. To extend the analysis far enough would have needed more experience and more knowledge than they could have possessed, together with more research and more work than they would have wished to undertake. If, even today, we discover daily new species that had hitherto escaped all our observations, think how many must have eluded men who judged things on first sight! As for primary categories and the most general concepts, it is unnecessary to add that they must have escaped their notice. How, for instance, would these men have imagined or understood the words 'matter', 'mind', 'substance', 'mode', 'figure', 'movement', when our philosophers, who have been using them for such a long time, have the greatest trouble understanding them themselves; and when the ideas which those words denote, being purely metaphysical, have no models to be found in nature?

I shall stop with these first steps, and ask my critics to suspend their reading here in order to judge on the basis of the invention of physical substantives, which is the easiest part of language to invent, how far language still has to go before the thoughts of man can find expression in a coherent form, and be susceptible to public utterance so as to influence society. I beg my critics to reflect how much time and knowledge must have been required for the discovery of numbers (N), abstract words, aorists, and all the tenses of verbs, particles, syntax, the method of connecting prepositions, the forms of reasoning, and the whole logic of language. For myself, alarmed as I am at the increasing difficulties, and convinced of the almost demonstrable impossibility that languages could have been created and established by purely human means,[21] I leave to anyone who will undertake it, the discussion of the following difficult problem: Which was the more necessary, a society already established for the invention of language, or language already invented for the establishment of society?

But whatever these origins may be, we see at least from the small pains which nature has taken to unite man through mutual needs or to facilitate the use of speech how little she has prepared their sociability and how little she has contributed to what they have done to establish bonds among themselves. Indeed it is impossible to imagine why in the primitive state one man should have more need of another man than a monkey or a wolf has need of another of its own kind,[22] or, if such a need were assumed, to imagine what motive could induce the second man to supply it, and if so, how the two would agree between them the terms of the transaction. I know we are constantly being told that nothing is more miserable than man in the state of nature; and if it is true, as I think I have proved, that it is only after many centuries that man could have had either the desire or the opportunity to quit that state, this is a charge to bring against nature and not against him whom nature has so constituted. But if I understand correctly the term 'miserable', it is a word that has no meaning or signifies only a painful deprivation and state of suffering in body or soul. Now I would be pleased to have it explained to me what kind of misery can be that of a free being whose heart is at peace and whose body is in health? I ask which – civilized or natural life – is the more liable to become unbearable to those who experience it? We see around us people who nearly all complain and several of whom indeed deprive themselves of their existence as far as they are able; and the joint sanction of divine and human law hardly suffices to halt this disorder. I ask if anyone has ever heard of a savage in a condition of freedom even dreaming of complaining about his life and killing himself? Let it be judged with less pride on which side the real misery lies. Nothing, on the contrary could be as miserable as a savage man dazzled by enlightenment, tormented by passions, and arguing about a state different from his own. It is thanks to a very wise Providence that the faculties which were potential in him should have become actual only with the opportunity of using them, so that they were neither superfluous nor onerous before their time, nor late in appearing and useless when the need arose. In instinct alone man had all he needed for living in a state of nature; in cultivated reason he has what is necessary only for living in society.

It would seem at first glance that men in the state of nature, having no kind of moral relationships between them, or any known duties, could be neither good nor evil, and that they could have neither vices nor virtues; unless we took those words in a material sense and called 'vices' in the indiv lual those characteristics which might be injurious to his own preservation and 'virtues' those which might contribute to it, in which case we should have to call the man who least resists the impulses of nature the most virtuous. However, without departing from the ordinary meaning of the words, we should do well to suspend judgement of such a situation, and beware of our own prejudices, until we have considered, with the scales of impartiality in our hands, whether there are more virtues than vices to be found among civilized men, whether those men's virtues are more advantageous to them than their vices are injurious, whether the progress of their knowledge is an adequate compensation for the harm they do each other as they learn of the good they ought to do each other, and whether, all things weighed up, they would not be in a happier situation if they had neither evil to fear from anyone, nor good to hope for, instead of being subjected to a universal dependence and being obliged to accept everything from those who are not obliged themselves to give them anything.

Above all, let us not conclude with Hobbes[23] that man is naturally evil just because he has no idea of goodness, that he is vicious for want of any knowledge of virtue, that he always refuses to do his fellow-men services which he does not believe he owes them, or that on the strength of the right he reasonably claims to things he needs, he foolishly imagines himself to be the sole proprietor of the whole universe. Hobbes saw very clearly the defects of all modern definitions of natural right, but the conclusions he drew from his own definition show that his own concept of natural right is equally defective. Reasoning on his own principles, that writer ought to have said that the state of nature, being the state where man's care for his own preservation is least prejudicial to that of others, is the one most conducive to peace and the most suited to mankind. Hobbes said precisely the opposite as a result of introducing, illogically, into the savage man's care for his own preservation the need to satisfy a multitude of passions which are the product of society and which have made laws necessary. The wicked man, he said, is a robust child.[24] It remains to be seen whether man in a state of nature is this robust child. Even if we conceded as much to Hobbes, what would he conclude from it? That if this man were as dependent on others when he is robust as when he is feeble, there is no kind of excess to which he would not resort: that he would assault his mother when she was slow in giving him to suck, that he would strangle a younger brother who got in his way, or bite the leg of another if he was disturbed or bothered by him. But two conflicting suppositions are here being made about man in the state of nature: that he is robust and that he is dependent. Man is weak when he is dependent, and is set free before he is robust. Hobbes did not see that the same cause which prevents the savage from using his reason (as our jurists claim) prevents him at the same time from abusing his faculties (as Hobbes himself claims). Thus one could say that savages are not wicked precisely because they do not know what it is to be good; for it is neither the development of intelligence nor the restraint of the laws, but the calm of the passions and the ignorance of vice which prevents them from doing evil. *Tanto plus in illis proficit vitiorum ignoratio, quam in his cognitio virtutis.** There is, moreover, another principle which Hobbes failed to notice and which, having been given to man to soften in certain circumstances the ferocity of his pride (O), or before the birth of that pride, his desire for self-preservation, serves to moderate the ardour he has for his own wellbeing by giving him an innate repugnance against seeing a fellow creature suffer. I believe I need fear no contradiction in attributing to man the one natural virtue that the most extreme detractor of human virtue was forced to recognize. I speak of compassion, a disposition well suited to creatures as weak and subject to as many ills as we are, a virtue all the more universal, and all the more useful to man in that it comes before any kind of reflection, and is so natural a virtue that even beasts sometimes show perceptible signs of it. Without speaking of the tenderness of mothers for their young, and how they face dangers they incur in order to protect them, we observe every day the aversion of horses against trampling on any living body. An animal never passes the corpse of a creature of its own species without distress. There are even those which give their dead a sort of burial; and the mournful lowing of cattle entering a slaughter house reveals

* 'So far has ignorance of vice been more advantageous to the Scythians than knowledge of virtue to the Greeks', Justin, *Histories*, II, ii.

their feelings in witnessing the horrible spectacle that confronts them. One sees with pleasure how the author of *The Fable of the Bees*,[25] when forced to acknowledge that man is a creature of compassion and feeling, discards his cold and sophisticated style in the example he gives of this, offering us the heartrending image of a man being compelled to observe, from a place of imprisonment, a wild beast tear a child from his mother's breast, crush the child's frail limbs with its murderous teeth and tear out the living entrails with its claws. What terrible agitation must be felt by this witness of an event in which he has no personal interest! What anguish he must suffer in seeing it and being unable to do anything to help the fainting mother or the dying child!

Such is the pure movement of nature, prior to all reflection; such is the force of natural pity, which the utmost depravity of morals is hardly able to destroy – for we see daily in our theatres men being moved, even weeping at the sufferings of a wretch who, were they in the tyrant's place would only increase the torments of his enemy.* Mandeville well realized that men, despite all their morality, would never have been any better than monsters if nature had not given them pity to support reason, but he failed to see that all the social virtues which he denies in men flow from this quality alone. In fact, what are generosity, mercy and humanity but compassion applied to the weak, to the guilty or to the human race in general? Benevolence, and even friendship, correctly understood, is only the outcome of constant compassion directed towards a particular object; for is desiring that a person should not suffer other than desiring that he should be happy? Even if it were true that pity is no more than a feeling that puts us in the place of the sufferer,[26] a feeling that is obscure but strong in savage man, and developed but weak in civilized man, what difference would this make to my argument, except to give it

---

* They are like the bloodthirsty Sulla, who was so sensitive to sufferings he had not caused, or like Alexander of Pherae, who did not dare attend the performance of any tragedy, lest he be seen sobbing with Andromache and Priam, although he could listen without emotion to the cries of all the citizens whose throats were cut daily on his orders: 'Tenderness of heart is the gift Nature declares she gave to the human race with the gift of tears'

(*Mollissima corda
Humano generi dare se natura fatetur
Quae lacrimas dedit*)
Juvenal, *Satires*, XV, 131 [Added to Edition of 1782].

more force? In fact, pity becomes all the more intense as the perceiving animal identifies itself more intimately with the suffering animal. Now it is clear that this identification must have been infinitely closer in the state of nature than in the state of reasoning. It is reason which breeds pride[27] and reflection which fortifies it; reason which turns man inward into himself; reason which separates him from everything which troubles or affects him. It is philosophy which isolates a man, and prompts him to say in secret at the sight of another suffering: 'Perish if you will; I am safe.' No longer can anything but dangers to society in general disturb the tranquil sleep of the philosopher or drag him from his bed. A fellow-man may with impunity be murdered under his window, for the philosopher has only to put his hands over his ears and argue a little with himself to prevent nature, which rebels inside him, from making him identify himself with the victim of the murder.[28] The savage man entirely lacks this admirable talent, and for want of wisdom and reason he always responds recklessly to the first promptings of human feeling. In riots or fights in the streets it is always the populace that gathers round; the prudent man departs; it is the ill-bred mob, the market-women who separate the combatants and prevent superior people from killing one another.

It is therefore very certain that pity is a natural sentiment which, by moderating in each individual the activity of self-love, contributes to the mutual preservation of the whole species. It is pity which carries us without reflection to the aid of those we see suffering; it is pity which in the state of nature takes the place of laws, morals and virtues, with the added advantage that no one there is tempted to disobey its gentle voice; it will always dissuade a robust savage from robbing a weak child or a sick old man of his hard-won sustenance if he has hope of finding his own elsewhere; it is pity which, in place of that noble maxim of rational justice 'Do unto others as you would have them do unto you', inspires all men with this other maxim of natural goodness, much less perfect but perhaps more useful: 'Do good to yourself with as little possible harm to others.' In a word, it is to this natural feeling, rather than to subtle arguments, that we must look for the origin of that repugnance which every man would feel against doing evil, even independently of the maxims of education. Although it may be proper for Socrates and other minds of that class to acquire virtue through reason, the human race would long since have ceased to exist if its preservation had depended only on the reasoning of the individuals who compose it.

When men had such inactive passions, and such a salutary curb, when they were wild rather than wicked, and more intent on protecting themselves from the harm that might be done to them than tempted to do harm to others, they were not prone to especially dangerous quarrels.[29] Since they had no kind of intercourse with one another, and had in consequence no experience of vanity, consideration, esteem or contempt; since they had not the least idea of *meum* and *tuum*, or any authentic idea of justice; and since they regarded any violence they might suffer as an injury easily healed rather than an insult to be punished; and since they did not even dream of vengeance, except perhaps mechanically and on the spot, like a dog that bites a stone thrown at him, these men's disputes would seldom have had bloody consequences, provided there was no more sensitive subject than food: and yet I see a more dangerous subject, of which it remains for me to speak.

Among the passions that agitate the heart of man, there is one, ardent and impetuous, which renders the sexes necessary to each other, a terrible passion which braves all dangers, defies all obstacles, and which in its fury seems liable to destroy the very human race it is meant to preserve. What must become of men, who are prey to this unrestrained and brutal rage, without shame, without modesty, fighting every day over their loves at the cost of their blood?

At first it must be agreed that the more violent the passions, the more necessary are laws to restrain them; but the disorders and crimes which these passions cause every day among us demonstrate well enough the inadequacy of laws to achieve this end; and, what is more, it would be worth considering whether these disorders did not arise with the laws themselves, in which case, if the laws were capable of suppressing anything, the very least that ought to be demanded of them is that they should put an end to an evil which would not exist without them.

Let us begin by distinguishing the moral from the physical in the sentiment of love. The physical is that general desire which propels one sex to unite with the other; the moral is that which shapes this desire and fixes it exclusively on one particular object, or at least gives the desire for this chosen object a greater degree of energy. Now it is easy to see that the moral part of love is an artificial sentiment, born of usage in society, and cultivated by women with much skill and care in order to establish their empire over men, and so make dominant the sex that ought to obey.[30] This sentiment, being based on certain notions of merit and beauty that a savage is incapable of having, and on comparisons he is incapable of making, must be for him almost non-existent. For since his mind cannot form abstract ideas of regularity and proportion, his heart is not capable of feeling those sentiments of love and admiration which – even if unconsciously – arise from the application of these ideas: he responds only to the temperament which nature has implanted in him, and not to taste (or distaste*), which he has not been able to acquire: for him every woman is good.

Confined solely to the physical part of love, and fortunate enough to be ignorant of those preferences which stimulate the appetite while increasing the difficulties of satisfying it, men must experience the ardours of their temperament less frequently and less vividly and consequently have fewer and less cruel quarrels. Imagination, which causes so much havoc among us, never speaks to the heart of savages;[31] everyone quietly awaits the impulse of nature, responds to it involuntarily with more pleasure than frenzy; and once the need is satisfied, all desire is extinguished.

It is therefore an incontestable fact that it is only in society that even love, together with all the other passions, has acquired that impetuous ardour which so often renders it fatal to men; and it is all the more ridiculous to depict savages endlessly killing each other to satisfy their brutality, since this image is directly contrary to experience; the Caribs, who of all peoples existing today have least departed from the state of nature, are precisely the most peaceful in their loves, and the least subject to jealousy, despite their living in the kind of hot climate which always seems to inflame those passions.

As for the inferences one might draw from obscurity several species of animals, from the combats of males which soil our farmyards at all seasons with blood or make our forests resound in spring with their cries as they dispute over females, we must begin by excluding all those species where nature has manifestly established, through the relative strengths of the sexes, relationships different from ours. Fights

---

*[Edition of 1782.]

between cocks, therefore, provide no basis for any inference about the human species. In those species where the proportions are more balanced, such conflicts can only be caused by a scarcity of females in comparison to the number of males, or to the periods of exclusion, when the female constantly refuses the approach of the male, which amounts to the same thing as the scarcity, for if each female accepts the male only during two months of the year, it is as if the population of females had been reduced by five-sixths. Now, neither of these two cases is applicable to the human species, where the number of females generally exceeds that of males,[32] and where no one has ever observed, even among savages, females having like those other species, fixed periods of heat and exclusion. Moreover, among several of such animals, the whole species goes on heat at the same time, so that there comes a terrible moment of universal passion, a moment that does not occur in the human species, where love is never seasonal. Therefore one cannot draw any inference about men in the state of nature from the fights that take place among certain animals for the possession of the female; and even if we could make such an inference, the fact that these conflicts do not destroy the species, obliges us to believe that they would not be more fatal to ours; and it is very obvious that they would still cause less havoc in the state of nature than they do in society, particularly in those countries where, morals still counting for something, the jealousy of lovers and the vengeance of husbands are the daily cause of duels, murders and even worse deeds, and where the duty of eternal fidelity serves only to produce adulterers, and where the laws of continence and honour necessarily themselves increase debauchery and multiply abortions.

We conclude,[33] then, that savage man, wandering in the forests, without work, without speech, without a home, without war, and without relationships, was equally without any need of his fellow men and without any desire to hurt them, perhaps not even recognizing any one of them individually. Being subject to so few passions, and sufficient unto himself, he had only such feelings and such knowledge as suited his condition; he felt only his true needs, saw only what he believed it was necessary to see, and his intelligence made no more progress than his vanity. If by chance he made some discovery, he was all the less able to communicate it to others because he did not even recognize his own children. Every art would perish with the inventor. There was neither education nor progress; the generations multiplied uselessly, and as each began afresh from the same starting-point, centuries rolled on as underdeveloped as the first ages; the species was already old, and man remained eternally a child.

If I have dwelled so long on the hypothesis of this primitive condition, it is because, having ancient errors and inveterate prejudices to eliminate, I thought I ought to dig down to the roots, and provide a picture of the true state of nature, to show to what extent inequality, even in its natural form, is far from having in that state as much reality and influence as our writers claim.

In fact, it is easy to see that among the differences which distinguish between men that several are taken to be natural which are solely the product of habit and of the various ways of life that man adopts in society. Thus a robust or a delicate temperament, together with the strength or weakness attaching to it, often derives from the manly or the effeminate manner in which one has been raised rather than from the original constitution of the body. The same is true of the powers of the mind; and not only does education establish a difference between cultivated minds and those which are not, but it increases the differences among cultivated minds in proportion to their culture; for when a giant and a dwarf walk the same road, every step each takes gives an extra advantage to the giant. Now if we compare the prodigious diversity of upbringings and of ways of life which prevail among the different classes in the civil state with the simplicity and uniformity of animal and savage life, where everyone eats the same foods, lives in the same style and does exactly the same things, it will be understood how much less the difference between man and man must be in the state of nature than it is in society, and how much natural inequality must be increased in the human species through the effects of instituted inequality.

But even if nature did exhibit in the distribution of her gifts as much partiality as is claimed, what advantage would the most favoured draw from it, to the detriment of the others, in a state of affairs which permitted almost no relationship between persons? There, where there is no love, what would be the use of beauty?[34] What is intelligence to people who do not speak, or cunning to those who have no commerce with others? I hear it constantly repeated that the stronger will oppress the weak, but I would like someone to explain to me what is meant by the word 'oppression'. Does it mean some men dominating with violence, and others groaning in slavish submission to their whims? Such is precisely what I observe among us, but I do not see how the same situation could be attributed to savage men, who could hardly even be brought to understand what servitude and domination are. A savage may well seize the fruits which another has gathered, seize the game he has killed, or the cave he is using as his shelter; but how will he ever be able to exact obedience? And what sort of chains of dependence could exist among men who possess nothing? I am chased from one tree, I am free to go to the next; if I am tormented in one place, who will prevent my moving somewhere else? Is there a man who is so much stronger than me and who is, moreover, depraved enough, lazy enough and fierce enough to compel me to provide for his sustenance while he remains idle? He must resolve not to lose sight of me for a single moment, and keep me very carefully bound while he sleeps, for fear that I should escape or kill him: that is to say, he is obliged to expose himself voluntarily to much worse trouble than the trouble he wishes to avoid, or gives to me. After all this, suppose his vigilance slackens for a moment? An unexpected noise makes him turn his head? I slip twenty paces into the forest, my chains are broken, and he will never see me again in his life.

Without expanding uselessly on these details, anyone must see that since the bonds of servitude are formed only through the mutual dependence of men and the reciprocal needs that unite them, it is impossible to enslave a man without first putting him in a situation where he cannot do without another man, and since such a situation does not exist in the state of nature, each man there is free of the yoke, and the law of the strongest is rendered vain.

Having proved that inequality is hardly perceived in the state of nature, and that its influence there is almost nil, it remains for me to explain its origin and its progress in the successive developments of the human mind. After having shown that *improvability*,[35] the social virtues and other faculties that natural man received as potentialities could never have developed by themselves, that in order to develop they needed the fortuitous concurrence of several alien causes which might never have arisen and without which man would have remained forever in his primitive condition, I must now consider and bring together the different chance factors which have succeeded in improving human reason while worsening the human species, making man wicked while making him sociable, and carrying man and the world from their remote beginnings to the point at which we now behold them.

Since the events I have to describe might have happened in several ways, I admit I can make the choice between those possibilities only by means of conjecture: but beside the fact that those conjectures become rational when they are the most probable that can be inferred from the nature of things and constitute the only means one can have for discovering the truth, the conclusions I want to deduce from mine will not thereby be conjectural, since, on the basis of the principles I have established, it would be impossible to formulate any other system which would not yield the same results and from which I could not draw identical conclusions.

This will exempt me from elaborating my thoughts about the way in which the passage of time makes up for the slender probability of events, or about the surprising potency of very trivial causes when they operate without interruption; or about the impossibility, on the one hand, of demolishing certain hypotheses, and, on the other hand, of giving them the measure of certainty of facts; or again about how, when two facts given as real are to be connected by a series of intermediary facts which are either unknown or regarded as unknown, it is for history, when it exists, to furnish the facts that do connect them, and when history cannot, for philosophy to determine the kind of facts that might connect them. Finally, I will be excused from considering how similarity, in reference to events, reduces facts to a much smaller number of different classes than is usually imagined. It is enough for me to offer these subjects for the consideration of my critics; it is enough for me also to have set things out in such a way that the common reader has no need to consider them at all.

PART TWO

THE first man who, having enclosed a piece of land, thought of saying 'This is mine' and found people simple enough to believe him, was the true founder of civil society. How many crimes, wars, murders; how much misery and horror the human race would have been spared if someone had pulled up the stakes and filled in the ditch and cried out to his fellow men: 'Beware of listening to this impostor. You are lost if you forget that the fruits of the earth belong to everyone and that the earth itself belongs to no one!'[1] But it is highly probable that by this time things had reached a point beyond which they could not go on as they were; for the idea of property, depending on many prior ideas which could only have arisen in successive stages, was not formed all at once in the human mind.[2] It was necessary for men to make much progress, to acquire much industry and knowledge, to transmit and increase it from age to age, before arriving at this final stage of the state of nature. Let us therefore look farther back, and try to review from a single perspective the slow succession of events and discoveries in their most natural order.

Man's first feeling was that of his existence, his first concern was that of his preservation. The products of the earth furnished all the necessary aids; instinct prompted him to make use of them. While hunger and other appetites made him experience in turn different modes of existence, there was one appetite which urged him to perpetuate his own species: and this blind impulse, devoid of any sentiment of the heart, produced only a purely animal act. The need satisfied, the two sexes recognized each other no longer, and even the child meant nothing to the mother, as soon as he could do without her.

Such was the condition of nascent man; such was the life of an animal limited at first to mere sensation; and scarcely profiting from the gifts bestowed on him by nature, let alone was he dreaming of wresting anything from her. But difficulties soon presented themselves and man had to learn to overcome them. The height of trees, which prevented him from reaching their fruits; the competition of animals seeking to nourish themselves on the same fruits; the ferocity of animals who threatened his life – all this obliged man to apply himself to bodily exercises; he had to make himself agile, fleet of foot, and vigorous in combat. Natural weapons – branches of trees and stones – were soon found to be at hand. He learned to overcome the obstacles[3] of nature, to fight when necessary against other animals, to struggle for his subsistence even against other men, or to indemnify himself for what he was forced to yield to the stronger.

To the extent that the human race spread, men's difficulties multiplied with their numbers. Differences between soils, climates, and seasons would have forced men to adopt different ways of life. Barren years, long hard winters, scorching summers consuming everything, demanded new industry from men. Along the sea coast and river banks they invented the hook and line to become fishermen and fish eaters. In the forests they made bows and arrows, and became hunters and warriors. In cold countries they covered themselves with the skins of the beasts they killed. Lightning, a volcano, or some happy accident introduced them to fire – a fresh resource against the rigour of winter. They learned to conserve this element, then to reproduce it, and finally to use it to cook the meats they had previously eaten raw.

This repeated employment of entities distinct from himself and distinct from each other must naturally have engendered in men's minds the perception of certain relationships. Those relationships which we express by the words 'large', 'small', 'strong', 'weak', 'fast', 'slow', 'fearful', 'bold', and other similar ideas, compared when necessary and almost unthinkingly, finally produced in him some kind of reflection, or rather a mechanical prudence which would indicate to him the precautions most necessary for his safety.

The new knowledge which resulted from this development increased his superiority over other animals by making him conscious of it. He practised setting snares for them; he outwitted them in a thousand ways, and though many animals might surpass him in strength of combat or in speed of running, he became in time the master of those that might serve him and the scourge of those that might hurt him. Thus the first look he directed into himself provoked his first stirring of pride; and while hardly as yet knowing how to distinguish between ranks, he asserted the priority of his species, and so prepared himself from afar to claim priority for himself as an individual.

Although his fellow men were not to him what they are to us, and although he had hardly any more dealings with them than he had with other animals, they were not forgotten in his observations. The resemblances which he learned with time to discern between them, his female and himself, led him to think of others which he did not actually perceive; and seeing that they all behaved as he himself would behave in similar circumstances, he concluded that their manner of thinking and feeling entirely matched his own; and this important truth, once well rooted in his mind, made him follow, by an intuition as sure as logic and more prompt, the best rules of conduct it was suitable to observe towards them for the sake of his own advantage and safety.

Instructed by experience that love of one's own wellbeing is the sole motive of human action, he found himself in a position to distinguish the rare occasions when common interest justified his relying on the aid of his fellows, and those even rarer occasions when competition should make him distrust them. In the first case, he united with them in a herd, or at most in a sort of free association that committed no one and which lasted only as long as the passing need which had brought it into being. In the second case, each sought to grasp his own advantage, either by sheer force, if he believed he had the strength, or by cunning and subtlety if he felt himself to be the weaker.

In this way men could have gradually acquired some crude idea of mutual commitments, and of the advantages of fulfilling them; but only so far as present and perceptible interests might demand, for men had no foresight whatever, and far from troubling about a distant future, they did not even think of the next day. If it was a matter of hunting a deer, everyone well realized that he must remain faithfully at his post; but if a hare happened to pass within the reach of one of them, we cannot doubt that he would have gone off in pursuit of it without scruple and, having caught his own prey, he would have cared very little about having caused his companions to lose theirs.

It is easy to understand that such intercourse between them would not demand a language much more sophisticated than that of crows or monkeys, which group together in much the same way. Inarticulate cries, many gestures and some imitative noises must have been for long the universal human language; the addition to this in each country of certain articulated and conventional sounds (the institution of which, I have already said[3], is none too easy to explain) produced particular languages, crude and imperfect, rather like those we find today among various savage nations. I pass in a flash over many centuries, pressed by the brevity of time, the abundance of the things I have to say, and by the almost imperceptible progress of the first stages – for the more slowly the events unfolded, the more speedily they can be described.[4]

Those first slow developments finally enabled men to make more rapid ones. The more the mind became enlightened, the more industry improved. Soon, ceasing to doze under the first tree, or to withdraw into caves, men discovered that various sorts of hard sharp stones could serve as hatchets to cut wood, dig the soil, and make huts out of branches, which they learned to cover with clay and mud. This was the epoch of a first revolution, which established and differentiated families, and which introduced property of a sort from which perhaps even then many quarrels and fights were born. However, as the strongest men were probably the first to build themselves huts which they felt themselves able to defend, it is reasonable to believe that the weak found it quicker and safer to imitate them rather than try to dislodge them; and as for those who already possessed huts, no one would readily venture to appropriate his neighbour's, not so much because it did not belong to him as because it would be no use to him and because he could not seize it without exposing himself to a very lively fight with the family which occupied it.

The first movements of the heart were the effect of this new situation, which united in a common dwelling husbands and wives, fathers and children; the habit of living together generated the sweetest sentiments known to man, conjugal love and paternal love. Each family became a little society, all the better united because mutual affection and liberty were its only bonds; at this stage also the first differences were established in the ways of life of the two sexes which had hitherto been identical. Women became more sedentary and accustomed themselves to looking after the hut and the children while men went out to seek their common subsistence. The two sexes began, in living a rather softer life, to lose something of their ferocity and their strength; but if each individual became separately less able to fight wild beasts, all, on the other hand, found it easier to group together to resist them jointly.

This new condition, with its solitary and simple life, very limited in its needs, and very few instruments invented to supply them, left men to enjoy a great deal of leisure, which they used to procure many sorts of commodities unknown to their fathers; and this was the first yoke they imposed on themselves, without thinking about it, and the first source of the evils they prepared for their descendants. For not only did such commodities continue to soften both body and mind, they almost lost through habitual use their power to please, and as they had at the same time degenerated into actual needs, being deprived of them became much more cruel than the possession of them was sweet; and people were unhappy in losing them without being happy in possessing them.

Here one can see a little more clearly how the use of speech became established and improved imperceptibly in the bosom of each family, and one might again speculate as to how particular causes could have extended and accelerated the progress of language by making language more necessary. Great floods or earthquakes surrounded inhabited districts with seas or precipices; revolutions of the globe broke off portions of continents into islands. One imagines that among men thus brought together, and forced to live together, a common tongue must have developed sooner than it would among those who still wandered freely through the forests of the mainland. Thus it is very possible that islanders, after their first attempts at navigation, brought the use of speech to us; and it is at least very probable that society and languages were born on islands and perfected there before they came to the continent.

Everything begins to change its aspect. Men who had previously been wandering around the woods, having once adopted a fixed settlement, come gradually together, unite in different groups, and form in each country a particular nation, united by customs and character – not by rules and laws, but through having a common way of living and eating and through the common influence of the same climate. A permanent proximity cannot fail to engender in the end some relationships between different families. Young people of opposite sexes live in neighbouring huts; and the transient intercourse demanded by nature soon leads, through mutual frequentation, to another kind of relationship, no less sweet and more permanent.[5] People become accustomed to judging different objects and to making comparisons; gradually they acquire ideas of merit and of beauty, which in turn produce feelings of preference. As a result of seeing each other, people cannot do without seeing more of each other. A tender and sweet sentiment insinuates itself into the soul, and at the least obstacle becomes an inflamed fury; jealousy awakens with love; discord triumphs, and the gentlest of passions receives the sacrifice of human blood.[6]

To the extent that ideas and feelings succeeded one another, and the heart and mind were exercised, the human race became more sociable, relationships became more extensive and bonds tightened. People grew used to gathering together in front of their huts or around a large tree; singing and dancing, true progeny of love and leisure, became the amusement, or rather the occupation, of idle men and women thus assembled. Each began to look at the others and to want to be looked at himself; and public esteem came to be prized. He who sang or danced the best; he who was the most handsome, the strongest, the most adroit or the most eloquent became the most highly regarded, and this was the first step towards inequality and at the same time towards vice. From those first preferences there arose, on the one side, vanity and scorn, on the other, shame and envy, and the fermentation produced by these new leavens finally produced compounds fatal to happiness and innocence.[7]

As soon as men learned to value one another and the idea of consideration was formed in their minds, everyone claimed a right to it, and it was no longer possible for anyone to be refused consideration without affront. This gave rise to the first duties of civility, even among savages: and henceforth every intentional wrong became an outrage, because together with the hurt which might result from the injury, the offended party saw an insult to his person which was often more unbearable than the hurt itself. Thus, as everyone punished the contempt shown him by another in a manner proportionate to the esteem he accorded himself, revenge became terrible, and men grew bloodthirsty and cruel. This is precisely the stage reached by most of the savage peoples known to us; and it is for lack of having sufficiently distinguished between different ideas and seen how far those peoples already are from the first state of nature that so many authors have hastened to conclude that man is naturally cruel and needs civil institutions to make him peaceable, whereas in truth nothing is more peaceable than man in his primitive state; placed by nature at an equal distance from the stupidity of brutes and the fatal enlightenment of civilized man, limited equally by reason and instinct to defending himself against evils which threaten him, he is restrained by natural pity from doing harm to anyone, even after receiving harm himself: for according to the wise Locke: 'Where there is no property, there is no injury.'[8]

But it must be noted that society's having come into existence and relations among individuals having been already established meant that men were required to have qualities different from those they possessed from their primitive constitution; morality began to be introduced into human actions, and each man, prior to laws, was the sole judge and avenger of the offences he had received, so that the goodness suitable to the pure state of nature was no longer that which suited nascent society; it was necessary for punishments to be more severe to the extent that opportunities for offence became more frequent; and the terror of revenge had to serve in place of the restraint of laws. Thus although men had come to have less fortitude, and their natural pity had suffered some dilution, this period of the development of human faculties, the golden mean[9] between the indolence of the primitive state and the petulant activity of our own pride, must have been the happiest epoch and the most lasting. The more we reflect on it, the more we realize that this state was the least subject to revolutions, and the best for man (P); and that man can have left it only as the result of some fatal accident, which, for the common good, ought never to have happened. The example of savages, who have almost always been found at this point of development, appears to confirm that the human race was made to remain there always; to confirm that this state was the true youth of the world, and that all subsequent progress has been so many steps in appearance towards the improvement of the individual, but so many steps in reality towards the decrepitude of the species.

As long as men were content with their rustic huts, as long as they confined themselves to sewing their garments of skin with thorns or fish-bones, and adorning themselves with feathers or shells, to painting their bodies with various colours, to improving or decorating their bows and arrows; and to using sharp stones to make a few fishing canoes or crude musical instruments; in a word, so long as they applied themselves only to work that one person could accomplish alone and tc :rts that did not require the collaboration of several hands, they lived as free, healthy, good and happy men so far as they could be according to their nature and they continued to enjoy among themselves the sweetness of independent intercourse; but from the instant one man needed the help of another, and it was found to be useful for one man to have provisions enough for two, equality disappeared, property was introduced, work became necessary, and vast forests were transformed into pleasant fields which had to be watered with the sweat of men, and where slavery and misery were soon seen to germinate and flourish with the crops.

Metallurgy and agriculture were the two arts whose invention produced this great revolution. For the poet it is gold and silver, but for the philosopher it is iron and wheat which first civilized men and ruined the human race. Both metallurgy and agriculture were unknown to the savages of America, who have always therefore remained savages;[10] other peoples seem to have remained barbarians, practising one of these arts and not the other; and one of the best reasons why Europe, if not the earliest to be civilized, has been at least more continuously and better civilized than other parts of the world, is perhaps that it is at once the richest in iron and the most fertile in wheat.[11]

It is very difficult to suggest how men came first to know and to use iron; for it is impossible to believe they would think on their own of drawing ore from the mine and undertaking the necessary preparations for smelting before they knew what the outcome would be. On the other hand, we can even less easily attribute this discovery to some accidental fire, since mines are formed only in barren places, denuded of trees and plants, so that one might say that nature had taken pains to hide this deadly secret from us.[12] There remains, therefore, only the faint possibility of some volcano, by pouring out metallic substances in fusion giving those who witnessed it the idea of imitating this operation of nature. What is more, we would have to assume those men having enough courage to undertake such arduous labour and enough foresight to envisage from afar the advantages they might derive from it – an assumption hardly to be made even of minds more developed than theirs.

As for agriculture, the principle of it was known long before the practice of it was established, and it is indeed hardly conceivable that men who were ceaselessly occupied drawing their subsistence from trees and plants did not fairly promptly acquire an idea of the means used by nature to propagate plants. Even so men's industry probably turned in that direction only very late – possibly because trees, which together with hunting and fishing provided their food, needed no husbandry, or because men had no knowledge of the use of wheat, or because they had no implements for cultivating it, or for lack of foresight into future needs, or, finally, for lack of the means of preventing others taking possession of the fruits of their labour. As soon as they became more skilled, we can believe that men began, with sharp stones and pointed sticks, to cultivate a few vegetables or roots around their huts;[13] although it was long before they knew how to process wheat or had the implements necessary for large-scale cultivation; they had also to learn that in order to devote oneself to that activity and sow seeds in the soil, one must resign oneself to an immediate loss for the sake of a greater gain in the future – a forethought very alien to the turn of mind of the savage man, who, as I have said, is hard pressed to imagine in the morning the needs he will have in the evening.

The invention of other arts must therefore have been necessary to compel the human race to apply itself to agriculture. As soon as some men were needed to smelt and forge iron, other men were needed to supply them with food.[14] The more the number of industrial workers multiplied, the fewer hands were engaged in providing the common subsistence, without there being any fewer mouths to consume it; and as some men needed commodities in exchange for their iron, others finally learned the secret of using iron for the multiplication of commodities. From this arose, on the one hand, ploughing and agriculture, and, on the other, the art of working metals and of multiplying their uses.

From the cultivation of the land, its division necessarily followed, and from property once recognized arose the first rules of justice: for in order to render each his own, each must be able to have something; moreover, as men began to direct their eyes towards the future and all saw that they had some goods to lose, there was no one who did not fear reprisals against himself for the injuries he might do to another. This origin is all the more natural, in that it is impossible to conceive of the idea of property arising from anything other than manual labour, for one cannot see what besides his own labour a man can add to things he has not actually made in order to appropriate them. It is his labour alone which, in giving the cultivator the right to the product of the land he has tilled, gives him in consequence the right to the land itself, at least until the harvest, which, being repeated from year to year, brings about a continued occupation, easily transformed into property. Grotius says that when the ancients gave Ceres the title of Legislatrix, and the festival celebrated in her honour the name of Thesmophoria, they implied that the division of the earth had produced a new sort of right: that is to say, the right to property different from the one derived from natural law.

Things in this state might have remained equal if talents had been equal, and if, for example, the use of iron and the consumption of foodstuffs had always exactly balanced each other, but this equilibrium, which nothing maintained, was soon broken: the stronger did more productive work, the more adroit did better work, the more ingenious devised ways of abridging his labour: the farmer had greater need of iron or the smith greater need of wheat, and with both working equally, the one earned plenty while the other had hardly enough to live on. It is thus that natural inequality merges imperceptibly with inequality of ranks, and the differences between men, increased by differences of circumstance, make themselves more visible and more permanent in their effects, and begin to exercise a correspondingly large influence over the destiny of individuals.

Things having once arrived at this point, it is easy to imagine the rest. I shall not pause to describe the successive invention of the other arts, the progress of language, the testing and employment of talents, the inequality of fortunes, the use and abuse of riches, and all the details which follow from this and which anyone can easily supply. I shall simply limit myself to casting a glance over the human race as it is placed in this new order of things.

Behold, then, all our faculties developed, memory and imagination brought into play, pride stimulated, reason made active and the mind almost at the point of the perfection of which it is capable. Behold all the natural qualities called into action, the rank and destiny of each man established, not only as to the quantity of his possessions and his power to serve or to injure, but as to intelligence, beauty, strength, skill, merit or talents; and since these qualities were the only ones that could attract consideration it soon became necessary either to have them or to feign them. It was necessary in one's own interest to seem to be other than one was in reality. Being and appearance became two entirely different things, and from this distinction arose insolent ostentation, deceitful cunning and all the vices that follow in their train.[15] From another point of view, behold man, who was formerly free and independent, diminished as a consequence of a multitude of new wants into subjection, one might say, to the whole of nature and especially to his fellow men, men of whom he has become the slave, in a sense, even in becoming their master; for if he is rich he needs their services; if he is poor he needs their aid; and even a middling condition does not enable him to do without them. He must therefore seek constantly to interest others in his lot and make them see an advantage, either real or apparent, for themselves in working for his benefit; all of which makes him devious and artful with some, imperious and hard towards others, and compels him to treat badly the people he needs if he cannot make them fear him and does not judge it in his interest to be of service to them. Finally, a devouring ambition, the burning passion to enlarge one's relative fortune, not so much from real need as to put oneself ahead of others, inspires in all men a dark propensity to injure one another, a secret jealousy which is all the more dangerous in that it often assumes the mask of benevolence in order to do its deeds in greater safety; in a word, there is competition and rivalry on the one hand, conflicts of interest on the other, and always the hidden desire to gain an advantage at the expense of other people. All these evils are the main effects of property and the inseparable consequences of nascent inequality.[16]

Before the invention of symbols to represent it, wealth could hardly consist of anything except land and livestock, the only real goods that men could possess. But when estates became so multiplied in number and extent as to cover the whole of the land and every estate to border on another one, no estate could be enlarged except at the expense of its neighbour; and the landless supernumeraries, whom weakness or indolence had prevented from acquiring an estate for themselves, became poor without having lost anything, because, while everything around them changed they alone remained unchanged, and so they were obliged to receive their subsistence – or to steal it – from the rich; and out of this situation there was born, according to the different characters of the rich and the poor, either dominion and servitude, or violence and robbery. The rich, for their part, had hardly learned the pleasure of dominating before they disdained all other pleasures, and using their old slaves to subdue new ones, they dreamed only of subjugating and enslaving their neighbours; like those ravenous wolves, which, having once tasted human flesh, refuse all other nourishment and desire thenceforth only to devour men.

Hence, as the strongest regarded their might, and the most wretched regarded their need as giving them a kind of right to the possessions of others, equivalent, according to them, to the right of property, the elimination of equality was followed by the most terrible disorder. The usurpations of the rich, the brigandage of the poor and the unbridled passions of everyone, stifling natural pity and the as yet feeble voice of justice, made men greedy, ambitious and bad. There arose between the right of the stronger and the right of the first occupant a perpetual conflict which ended only in fights and murders (Q). Nascent society gave place to the most horrible state of war; the human race, debased and desolate, could not now retrace its path, nor renounce the unfortunate acquisitions it had made, but labouring only towards its shame by misusing those faculties which should be its honour, brought itself to the brink of ruin.

> Shocked at a new-found evil, at once rich and wretched,
> He wants to flee from his wealth, and hates what he once prayed for.*
>
> [Ovid, *Metamorphosis*. XI. 127]

It is impossible that men should not eventually have reflected on so melancholy a situation, and on the calamity which had overwhelmed them. The rich above all must have perceived how disadvantageous to them was a perpetual state of war in which they bore all the costs, and in which the risk of life was universal but the risk of property theirs alone. Furthermore, whatever disguises they might put upon their usurpations, they knew well enough that they

---

* *Attonitus novitate mali, divesque miserque,*
  Effugere optat opes, et quae modo voverat, odit.

were founded on precarious and bogus rights and that force could take away from them what force alone had acquired without their having any reason for complaint. Even those who had been enriched by their own industry could not base their right to property on much better titles. In vain would one say: 'I built this wall; I earned the right to this field by my own labour.' For 'Who gave you its extent and boundaries?' might be the answer. 'And in virtue of what do you claim payment from us for work we never instructed you to do? Do you not know that a multitude of your brethren perish or suffer from need of what you have to excess, and that you required the express and unanimous consent of the whole human race in order to appropriate from the common subsistence anything beyond that required for your own subsistence?' Destitute of valid reasons to justify himself and of forces adequate to defend himself; easily crushing an individual but crushed himself by troupes of bandits; alone against all, and unable because of mutual jealousies to form alliances with his equals against enemies united by the common hope of plunder, the rich man under pressure of necessity conceived in the end the most cunning project that ever entered the human mind: to employ in his favour the very forces of those who attacked him, to make his adversaries his defenders, to inspire them with new maxims and give them new institutions as advantageous to him as natural right was disadvantageous.

To this end, having demonstrated to his neighbours the horror of a situation which set each against all, made men's possessions as burdensome to them as their needs, and afforded no security either in poverty or in riches, he invents specious reasons to lead his listeners to his goal.

'Let us unite', he says, 'to protect the weak from oppression, to restrain the ambitious, and ensure for each the possession of what belongs to him; let us institute rules of justice and peace to which all shall be obliged to conform, without exception, rules which compensate in a way for the caprice of fortune by subjecting equally the powerful and the weak to reciprocal duties. In a word, instead of directing our forces against each other, let us unite them together in one supreme power which shall govern us all according to wise laws, protect and defend all the members of the association, repulse common enemies, and maintain us in everlasting concord.'

It needed much less than the equivalent of this speech to win round men so uncultivated and so easily seduced, especially as they had too many disputes to settle among themselves to be able to do without umpires, and too much avarice and ambition to be able to do for long without masters. All ran towards their chains believing that they were securing their liberty; for although they had reason enough to discern the advantages of a civil order, they did not have experience enough to foresee the dangers. Those most capable of predicting the abuses were precisely those who expected to profit from them; and even the wisest saw that men must resolve to sacrifice one part of their freedom in order to preserve the other, even as a wounded man has his arm cut off to save the rest of his body.[17]

Such was, or must have been, the origin of society and of laws, which put new fetters on the weak and gave new powers to the rich (R), which irretrievably destroyed natural liberty, established for all time the law of property and inequality, transformed adroit usurpation into irrevocable right, and for the benefit of a few ambitious men subjected the human race thenceforth to labour, servitude and misery.[18] It is easy to see how the foundation of one society made the establishment of all the rest unavoidable, and how, being faced with united forces, it was necessary for others to unite in turn. Societies, as they multiplied and spread, soon came to cover the whole surface of the earth, and it was no longer possible to find a single corner of the universe where one might free oneself from the yoke and withdraw one's head from beneath the sword, often precariously held, which every man saw perpetually hanging over him.[19] Positive law having thus become the common rule over citizens, there was room for natural law only as between the various societies where, under the name of international law, it was moderated by certain tacit conventions designed to make intercourse possible and to supplement natural compassion, which having lost as between society and society nearly all the force it had as between man and man, no longer dwells in any but a few great cosmopolitan souls, who, breaking through the imaginary barriers that separate peoples, and following the example of the Sovereign Being who created them, include the whole human race in their benevolence.[20]

The bodies politic, thus remaining in the state of nature in their relationship to each other, soon experienced the same disadvantages that had forced individuals to quit it; the state of nature proved indeed even more harmful to these large bodies than it had previously been for the individuals of whom they were composed. From this there arose wars between nations, battles, murders, reprisals which make nature tremble and offend reason, and all those horrible prejudices which count the honour of shedding human blood a virtue. The most decent men learned to regard the killing of their fellows as one of their duties; and in time men came to massacre one another by thousands without knowing why, committing more murders in a single day's battle and more atrocities in the sack of a single city than were committed in the state of nature throughout entire centuries over the whole face of the earth. Such are the first effects we note of the division of the human race into different societies. But let us return to their foundation.

I know that many have suggested other origins for political societies, such as conquest by the most powerful or the union of the weak; and the choice between these causes makes no difference to what I wish to establish. However, the one I have just outlined seems to me the most natural for the following reasons:

(1) In the first place, the right of conquest, being no true right in itself, cannot be the basis of any other right; the victor and the vanquished always remain towards each in the state of war, unless the conquered nation, with its freedom fully restored, voluntarily chooses its conqueror for its chief. Up to that point, whatever capitulations may have been made, the fact that they have no basis but violence and are therefore *ipso facto* null and void means that there cannot be on this hypothesis any authentic society or true body politic, nor any law but the law of the strongest.

(2) The words 'strong' and 'weak' are, in the second case, ambiguous; for during the interval between the establishment of the right to property or the right of the first occupant and the establishment of political government, the sense of these terms is better expressed by the words 'poor' and 'rich', since before the institution of laws a man can have had in effect no means of subjecting his equals other than by attacking their goods or making them a part of his own.

(3) The poor, having nothing to lose but their freedom, it would have been the utmost folly on their part to strip themselves voluntarily

of the only good they still possessed without gaining anything in exchange. The rich, on the contrary, being vulnerable, so to speak, in every part of their possessions, it was much easier to injure them; and it was necessary in consequence for them to take more precautions for their own protection; and finally it is reasonable to suppose a thing to have been invented by those to whom it was useful rather than by those to whom it was injurious.

Nascent government did not have a constant and regular form. The lack of wisdom and experience allowed only present inconveniences to be seen, and men thought of remedies for others only when they presented themselves. In spite of the endeavours of the wisest lawgivers, the political state always remained imperfect because it was almost entirely the product of chance; and since it began badly, time, while revealing the defects and suggesting remedies, could never repair the vices of the constitution. Constitutions were continually being patched up, when it was really necessary to begin by clearing the ground and removing the old materials, as Lycurgus did in Sparta in order to build a stable and lasting edifice. At first, society consisted only of a few general conventions which all the individuals committed themselves to observe, conventions of which the community made itself the guarantor towards each individual. Experience had to show how weak was such a constitution, how easy it was for law-breakers to avoid conviction or punishment for crimes of which the public alone was witness and judge. The laws had to be evaded in a thousand ways, inconveniences and disorders had to multiply constantly for men to be brought finally to think of entrusting the dangerous responsibility of public authority to certain individuals and committing to the magistrates the duty of securing obedience to the deliberations of the people. For to say that the chiefs were chosen before the union was instituted, and that ministers of laws existed before the laws themselves is to suggest something that does not deserve serious consideration.

It would be no more reasonable to believe that men threw themselves straightaway into the arms of an absolute master, unconditionally and irrevocably, and that the first idea which proud and unconquered men conceived for their common security was to rush headlong into slavery. Why, in fact, did they give themselves a superior if it was not for him to defend themselves against oppression, and to protect their possessions, their liberties and their lives, which are, so to speak, the constituent elements of their being? Now, since the worst thing that can happen to one in the relations between man and man is to find oneself at the mercy of another, would it not be contrary to common sense for men to surrender into the hands of a chief the only things they needed his help in order to preserve? What equivalent benefit could he offer them in return for the concession of so great a right? And if he had dared to demand it on the pretext of defending them, would he not promptly have received the reply recorded in the fable: 'What worse would the enemy do to us?'[21] It is therefore incontestable – and indeed the fundamental principle of all political right – that people have given themselves chiefs in order to defend their liberty and not to enslave them. 'If we have a prince,' said Pliny to Trajan, 'it is in order that he may preserve us from having a master.'[22]

Politicians utter the same sophisms about love of liberty that philosophers utter about the state of nature; on the strength of things that they see, they make judgements about very different things that they have not seen, and they attribute to men a natural propensity to slavery because they witness the patience with which slaves bear their servitude, failing to remember that liberty is like innocence and virtue: the value of it is appreciated only so long as one possesses it oneself, and the taste for it is lost as soon as one loses it. 'I know the delights of your country,' said Brasidas to a satrap, who was comparing the life of Sparta with that of Persepolis, 'but you cannot know the pleasures of mine.'

Even as an unbroken horse erects its mane, paws the ground with its hoof, and rears impetuously at the very approach of the bit, while a trained horse suffers patiently even the whip and spur, savage man will not bend his neck to the yoke which civilized man wears without a murmur; he prefers the most turbulent freedom to the most tranquil subjection. We must not, therefore, look to the degradation of enslaved peoples as a basis for judging man's natural disposition for or against servitude, but look rather to the prodigious achievements of all free peoples who have striven to protect themselves from oppression. I know that enslaved peoples do nothing but boast of the peace and repose they enjoy in their chains, and *miserrimam servitutem pacem appellant.** But when I see free peoples sacrificing pleasure, repose, wealth, power, even life itself for the sake of preserving that one good which is so disdained by those who have lost it; when I see animals, born free and hating captivity, breaking their heads against the bars of their prison; when I see multitudes of naked savages scorn European pleasures and brave hunger, fire, the sword and death simply to preserve their independence, I feel that it is not for slaves to argue about liberty.

As for paternal authority, from which several writers have derived absolute government and all society, it is enough, without invoking the refutations of Locke and Sidney, to notice that nothing on earth can be farther from the ferocious spirit of despotism than the gentleness of that authority which looks more to the advantage of he who obeys than to the interest of he who commands; to notice that by the law of nature the father is the master of the child only for such time as his help is necessary to him and that beyond this stage the two are equals, the son, becoming perfectly independent of his father, owing him only respect and not obedience, for gratitude is manifestly a duty which ought to be observed and not a right which can be claimed. Instead of saying that civil society derives from paternal power, we ought to say, on the contrary, that the latter derives its main force from the former. No individual was recognized as the father of several children until such time as they lived in families together and settled around him. The goods of the father, of which he is truly the master, are the ties which keep his children dependent on him, and he may choose to give them a share of his estate only to the extent that they have deserved it from him by constant deference to his will. But subjects are far from having some similar favour to expect from their despot, for in belonging, with all they possess, to him as his personal property – or at least being claimed by him as such – they are reduced to receiving from him as a favour whatever he leaves them of their own goods. He bestows justice when he robs them; and grace when he lets them live.

If we go on thus to examine facts in the light of right, we shall find no more substance than truth in the so-called 'voluntary establish-

* 'They call a state of wretched servitude a state of peace', Tacitus, *Histories*, IV. xvii.[23]

ment' of tyranny, and it would be difficult to prove the validity of any contract which bound only one of the parties, which gave everything to one and nothing to the other, and which could only be prejudicial to one contractant. This odious system is very far from being, even today, that of wise and good monarchs, especially of the kings of France, as we may see from several statements in their edicts, and particularly in the following passage from a celebrated statement published in 1667 in the name, and by order, of Louis XIV:

> Let it not therefore be said that the Sovereign is not subject to the laws of his State, since the contrary proposition is a truth of the law of nations, which flattery has sometimes denied but which true princes have defended as divine protectors of their states. How much more legitimate is it to say with the wise Plato that the perfect felicity of a kingdom consists in a prince being obeyed by his subjects, the prince obeying the law, and the law being just and always directed to the public good.

I shall not pause to consider whether since freedom is the noblest of man's faculties, it is not to degrade our nature, to put ourselves on the level of beasts enslaved by instinct, even to offend the Author of our being, to renounce without reserve the most precious of all His gifts and subject ourselves to committing all the crimes He has forbidden in order to please a cruel or impassioned master, nor whether that sublime Artisan would be more angered at seeing His finest work destroyed than at seeing it dishonoured.* I shall only ask by what right those who do not fear debasing themselves in this way have been able to subject succeeding generations to the same ignominy, and to renounce on behalf of their posterity things which were not derived from their generosity and without which life itself is a burden to all who are worthy of life?

Pufendorf[24] says that just as one transfers property to another by agreements and contracts, one can divest oneself of one's freedom in favour of another. This, it seems to me, is a very bad argument, for, first of all, the goods I alienate become something wholly foreign to me, and any abuse of them is a matter of indifference to me; while

---

* I shall disregard, if it is wished, the authority of Barbeyrac,[25] who follows Locke in asserting squarely that no one can sell his freedom to the extent of submitting himself to an arbitrary power which may use him as it fancies. *For that*, he adds, *would be to sell one's own life of which one is not the master* [Edition of 1782].

it is very important to me that my freedom is not abused, and I cannot lay myself open to becoming an instrument of crime without incurring the guilt for whatever crime I am forced to commit.[26] Besides, since the right to property is only conventional and of human institution, everyone may dispose at will of what he possesses; but this is not the case with the essential gifts of nature, such as life and liberty, which everyone is allowed to enjoy and of which it is at least doubtful whether anyone has the right to divest himself. By giving up liberty, a man degrades his being: by giving up life, he does his best to annihilate it, and since no temporal goods could compensate for the loss of either life or liberty, it would be an offence against both nature and reason to renounce them at any price whatever. But even if one could alienate one's liberty like one's goods, the difference would be very great in the case of one's children, who enjoy their father's goods only by transmission of his right to them, whereas their freedom is a gift they receive as men from nature, so that their parents had never had a right to divest them of it. Thus, just as it was necessary to do violence to nature to establish slavery, nature had to be altered to perpetuate that right, and jurists who have solemnly affirmed that the child of a slave will be born a slave have decided, in other words, that a man will not be born a man.

It therefore seems to me certain that governments did not originate in arbitrary power, which is only the final stage of the corruption of governments, and which brings them back in the end to that very law of the strongest which they were first introduced to remedy; even if they had begun in this way, such power, being in its nature illegitimate, could not serve as the basis for rights in society, nor consequently for the inequality instituted in society.

Without entering here into the research that needs yet to be undertaken into the nature of the fundamental pact of all government, I shall limit myself, following common opinion, to considering here the establishment of the body politic as a true contract between a people and the chiefs that people chooses, a contract whereby both parties commit themselves to observe the laws which are stipulated in its articles and which form the bonds of their union. The people having, on the subject of social relations, united all their wills into a single will, all the articles on which that will pronounces become so many fundamental laws obligatory on every member of the state without exception; and one of these laws regulates the choice and powers of the magistrates charged to watch over the execution of the other laws. This power extends to everything that can maintain the constitution without going so far as to change it. Added to this are honours, which make the laws and their ministers command respect, and prerogatives, which compensate the ministers personally for the hard work which good administration entails. The magistrate, on his side, binds himself to use the power entrusted to him only in accordance with the intentions of the constituents, to maintain each in the peaceful enjoyment of what belongs to him and at all times to prefer the public interest to his own advantage.

Before experience had demonstrated, or knowledge of the human heart had made men foresee the inevitable abuses of such a constitution, it must have appeared all the better insofar as those charged with watching over its preservation were those who had the greatest stake in it. For the magistrature and its rights being established solely upon the fundamental laws, the magistrates would cease to be legitimate as soon as the laws were destroyed; the people would no longer owe them obedience; and because it is not the magistrate but the law which constitutes the essence of the state, each individual would return by right to his natural liberty.

Given the least careful thought, one could find new reasons to confirm this point and to see from the very nature of the contract that it cannot be irrevocable, for if there were no superior power to secure the fidelity of the contracting parties, nor compel them to fulfil their reciprocal engagements, each party would remain sole judge of his own cause, and each would always have the right to renounce the contract as soon as he considered that the other had violated its conditions, or as soon as those conditions ceased to suit his pleasure. It would seem that the right of abdication can be founded on this principle. Now to consider only, as we do here, what is of human institution, if the magistrate, who has all the power in his hands and who appropriates all the advantages of the contract, enjoys nonetheless the right to renounce his authority, all the more reason is there for the people, who pay for all the faults of their chiefs, to have the right to renounce their dependence. However, the frightful dissensions and infinite disorders that this dangerous power would necessarily bring about show us better than anything else how much human governments needed a basis more solid than reason alone, and how necessary it was to the public repose that divine will should intervene to give the sovereign authority a sacred and inviolable character which stripped subjects of the fatal right of disposing of it. If religion had done men only this service it would be enough to impose on them the duty of adopting and cherishing religion, despite its abuses, since it saves men from even more bloodshed than fanaticism causes. But let us follow the thread of our hypothesis.

The different forms of government owe their origin to the greater or lesser differences which exist between individuals at the moment a government is instituted. Was one man eminent in power, virtue, riches, or influence? Then he alone was elected magistrate, and the state became monarchic. If several men, more or less equal among themselves, were superior to all the others, they were elected jointly, and formed an aristocracy. Where those whose fortunes and talents were less disproportionate, and who were less far removed from the state of nature, kept the supreme administration in common they formed a democracy. Time showed which of these forms was the most advantageous for men. Some remained subject to laws alone; others were soon obeying masters. Citizens wished to keep their liberty; subjects thought only of taking it away from their neighbours, unable to endure the prospect of others enjoying a thing they had ceased to enjoy themselves. In a word, on one side were riches and conquests; on the other, happiness and virtue.

In these various governments, all magistrates were originally elective; and where wealth did not conquer, preference was accorded to merit, which gives a natural authority, and to age, which gives experience in business and gravity in deliberations. The elders of the Hebrews, the Gerontes of Sparta, the Senate of Rome, and the very etymology of our word *seigneur*, show how old age was respected in the past. But the more often the choice fell on men advanced in age, the more often elections had to take place and the more the troublesome aspects of election made themselves felt; intrigues began, factions were formed, parties became embittered, civil wars broke out; in the end the blood of citizens was sacrificed for what was claimed to be the happiness of the state, and men were on the verge of relapsing into the anarchy of earlier times. Ambitious leaders took advantage of this situation to perpetuate their offices in their own families; at the same time, the people, accustomed to dependence, to repose and to the conveniences of life, and already incapable of breaking the chains it bore, agreed to allow its servitude to be increased for the sake of assuring its tranquillity. Thus, the chiefs in becoming hereditary accustomed themselves to thinking of their magistrates as a family possession, and to regarding themselves as proprietors of the state of which they were originally only the officers, to calling their co-citizens their slaves, and numbering them, like cattle, among their belongings, and to calling themselves the equals of the gods and the king of kings.

If we follow the progress of inequality in these different revolutions, we shall find that the establishment of law and the right of property was the first stage, the institution of magistrates the second, and the transformation of legitimate into arbitrary power the third and last stage. Thus, the status of rich and poor was authorized by the first epoch, that of strong and weak by the second, and by the third that of master and slave, which is the last degree of inequality, and the stage to which all the others finally lead until new revolutions dissolve the government altogether or bring it back to legitimacy.

To understand the necessity of this progress, we must consider less the motives for the establishment of the body politic than the way in which that body performs in action and the disadvantages it introduces, for the vices which make social institutions necessary are the same vices which make the abuse of those institutions inevitable.[27] Leaving aside the unique case of Sparta, where the laws concerned mainly the education of children and where Lycurgus established morals so well that it was almost unnecessary to add laws, laws, being in general less strong than passions, restrain men without changing them; so that it would be easy to prove that any government which, without being corrupted or degenerate, worked perfectly according to the ends of its institution, would have been instituted unnecessarily, and that a country where nobody evaded the laws or exploited the magistracy would need neither laws nor magistrates.

Political distinctions necessarily introduce civil distinctions. The growing inequality between the people and its chiefs is soon reproduced between individuals, and is modified there in a thousand ways according to passions, talents and circumstances. The magistrate cannot usurp illegitimate power without enrolling clients to whom he is forced to yield some part of it. Besides, citizens allow themselves to be oppressed only so far as they are impelled by a blind ambition; and fixing their eyes below rather than above themselves, come to love domination more than independence, and agree to wear chains for the sake of imposing chains on others in turn. It is difficult to reduce to obedience a man who has no wish to command, and the most adroit politician could not enslave men whose only wish was to be free; on the other hand, inequality extends easily among ambitious and cowardly souls, who are always ready to run the risks of fortune and almost indifferent as to whether they command or obey, according to fortune's favour. Thus there must have come a time when the eyes of the people were so dazzled that their leaders had only to say to the least of men: 'Be great, with all your posterity', and at once that man appeared great in the eyes of all the world as well as in his own eyes and his descendants exalted themselves all the more in proportion to their distance from him; the more remote and uncertain the cause, the greater the effect; the more idlers who could be counted in a family, the more illustrious it became.

If this were the place to go into details, I would explain how* inequality of influence and authority becomes inevitable among individuals (S) as soon as, being united in the same society, they are forced to compare themselves with one another and to take into account the differences they discover in the continual dealings they have with one another. These differences are of several kinds, but since wealth, nobility or rank, power and personal merit are generally the four principal qualities by which one is measured in society, I would prove that harmony or conflict between these several sorts of distinction is the surest indication of the good or bad constitution of a state. I would show that as between these four kinds of inequality, personal qualities are the origin of all the others, and wealth is the last to which they are all reduced because wealth, being the most immediately useful to wellbeing and the easiest to communicate, can be readily used to buy all the rest – an observation which enables us to judge fairly exactly how far each people has distanced itself from its primitive institution, and the progress it has made towards the extreme stage of corruption. I would observe to

---

* even without the intervention of government [Edition of 1782].

what extent this universal desire for reputation, honours and promotion, which devours us all, exercises and compares talents and strengths; I would show how it excites and multiplies passions, and how, in turning all men into competitors, rivals or rather enemies, it causes every day failures and successes and catastrophies of every sort by making so many contenders run the same course; I would show that this burning desire to be talked about,[28] this yearning for distinction which keeps us almost always in a restless state is responsible for what is best and what is worst among men, for our virtues and our vices, for our sciences and our mistakes, for our conquerors and our philosophers – that is to say, for a multitude of bad things and very few good things. Finally, I would prove that if one sees a handful of powerful and rich men on the pinnacle of grandeur and fortune, while the crowd grovels below in obscurity and wretchedness, it is because the former value the things they enjoy only to the extent that the others are deprived of them and because, even without changing their condition, they would cease to be happy if the people ceased to be miserable.[29]

However, these details alone would provide the material for a substantial work, in which the advantages and disadvantages of any government would be weighed in relation to the rights of the state of nature, and where one would strip all the different masks behind which inequality has hidden itself up to the present time and may do so in centuries to come, according to the nature of governments and the revolutions which time will necessarily produce in them. One would see the multitude oppressed inside society as a consequence of the very precautions taken against threats from outside; one would see oppression increase continually without the oppressed ever being able to know where it would end, nor what legitimate means remained for them to halt it. One would see the rights of citizens and the freedom of nations extinguished little by little, and the protests of the weak treated as seditious noises. One would see politics confer on a mercenary section of the people the honour of defending the common cause; one would see arising from this the necessity of taxation, and the disheartened farmer quitting his fields even in peacetime, abandoning his plough to buckle on the sword. One would see the birth of fatal and bizarre codes of honour. One would see the defenders of the fatherland become sooner or later its enemies, holding for ever a drawn dagger over their fellow citizens, soldiers who in time would be heard to say to the oppressor of their country:

> If you command me to sink my sword into my brother's breast, or in my father's throat, or even into the womb of my pregnant wife, I shall do it all, despite my repugnance, with my own right hand.
>
> Lucan, *Pharsalia*, I[30]

From the extreme inequality of conditions and fortunes, from the diversity of passions and talents, from useless arts, pernicious arts and foolish sciences would arise a mass of prejudices, equally contrary to reason, happiness and virtue; one would see chiefs fomenting everything that might weaken assemblies of men by disuniting them, stirring up everything that might give society an appearance of concord while sowing the seeds of real dissension, everything that might inspire defiance and mutual hatred in different social orders through conflict between their rights and their interests, and by these means strengthen the power which subdues them all.[31]

It is from the bosom of this disorder and these revolutions that despotism, by degrees raising up its hideous head and devouring everything that it had seen to be good and sound in any part of the state, would finally succeed in trampling on both the laws and the people and establishing itself on the ruins of the republic. The times leading up to these final changes would be times of troubles and calamities; but in the end all would be consumed by the monster, and the people would no longer have chiefs and laws, but only tyrants. After this moment also there would be no morals or virtue, for despotism, 'in which there is no hope to be derived from an honourable deed',[32] admits, wherever it prevails, no other master; and as soon as it speaks, there is neither probity nor duty to consult, and the blindest obedience is the solitary virtue which remains for slaves.

This is the last stage of inequality, and the extreme term which closes the circle and meets the point from which we started. It is here that all individuals become equal again because they are nothing, here where subjects have no longer any law but the will of the master, nor the master any other rule but that of his passions, here that notions of the good and principles of justice vanish once more. Here everything is restored to the sole law of the strongest, and consequently to a new state of nature different from the one with which we began only that that one was the state of nature in its pure form and this one is the fruit of an excess of corruption. There is so little difference, moreover, between the two states, and the contract of government is so fully dissolved by despotism that the despot is only master for as long as he is the strongest; as soon as he can be expelled, he has no right to protest against violence. The insurrection which ends with the strangling or dethronement of a sultan is just as lawful an act as those by which he disposed the day before of the lives and property of his subjects. Force alone maintained him; force alone overthrows him; all things happen according to the natural order; and whatever the result of these short and frequent revolutions, no man can complain of the injustice of another, but only of his own imprudence or his misfortune.

In thus discovering and tracing the lost and forgotten paths which must have led men from the natural state to the civil state, in reconstructing together with the intermediate situations which I have just noted, those which lack of time has made me omit or which imagination has not suggested to me, no attentive reader can fail to be impressed by the immense space which separates these two states. It is in this slow succession of things that he will see the solution to an infinity of moral and political problems which philosophers cannot solve. He will understand that since the human race of one age is not the human race of another age, the reason why Diogenes could not find a man is that he searched among his contemporaries for a man of a time that no longer existed; Cato, he will say, perished with Rome and liberty because he was out of place in his century, and the greatest of men could only astound the world that he would have ruled five centuries earlier. In a word, the attentive reader will explain how the soul and the human passions through imperceptible degeneration change, so to speak, their nature; explain why our needs and our pleasures change their objects in the long run; and why since original man has disappeared by degrees, society no longer offers to the eyes of philosophers anything more than an assemblage of artificial men and factitious passions which are the product of all men's new relations and which have no true foundation in nature. What reflection teaches on this subject is perfectly confirmed by observation; savage man and civilized man differ so much in the bottom of their hearts and inclinations that that which constitutes the supreme happiness of the one would reduce the other to despair. The savage man breathes only peace and freedom; he desires only to live and stay idle, and even the *ataraxia* of the Stoic does not approach his profound indifference towards every other object. Civil man, on the contrary, being always active, sweating and restless, torments himself endlessly in search of ever more laborious occupations; he works himself to death, he even runs towards the grave to put himself into shape to live, or renounces life in order to acquire immortality. He pays court to great men he loathes and to rich men he despises; he spares nothing to secure the honour of serving them; he boasts vaingloriously of his own baseness and of their patronage, and being proud of his slavery he speaks with disdain of those who have not the honour of sharing it. What a spectacle for a Carib would be the arduous and envied labours of a European minister! How many cruel deaths would not that indolent savage prefer to the horrors of such a life, which often is not even sweetened by the satisfaction of doing good? In order for him to understand the motives of anyone assuming so many cares, it would be necessary for the words 'power' and 'reputation' to have a meaning for his mind; he would have to know that there is a class of men who attach importance to the gaze of the rest of the world, and who know how to be happy and satisfied with themselves on the testimony of others rather than on their own. Such is, in fact, the true cause of all these differences: the savage lives within himself; social man lives always outside himself;[33] he knows how to live only in the opinion of others, it is, so to speak, from their judgement alone that he derives the sense of his own existence. It is not my subject here to show how such a disposition gives birth to so much indifference to good and evil coupled with such beautiful talk about morality; or how, as everything is reduced to appearances, everything comes to be false and warped, honour, friendship, virtue, and often even vices themselves, since in the end men discover the secret of boasting about vices; or show how, as a result of always asking others what we are and never daring to put the question to ourselves in the midst of so much philosophy, humanity, civility and so many sublime maxims, we have only façades, deceptive and frivolous, honour without virtue, reason without wisdom, and pleasure without happiness. It is enough for me to have proved that this is not at all the original state of men, and that it is only the spirit of society together with the inequality that society engenders which changes and corrupts in this way all our natural inclinations.

I have tried to set out the origin and progress of inequality, the establishment and the abuse of political societies, to the extent that these things can be deduced from the nature of man by the light of reason alone, independently of the sacred dogmas which give to sovereign authority the sanction of divine right. It follows from this exposition that inequality, being almost non-existent in the state of nature, derives its force and its growth from the development of our faculties and the progress of the human mind, and finally becomes fixed and legitimate through the institution of property and laws. It follows furthermore that that moral inequality, authorized by positive law alone, is contrary to natural right, whenever it is not matched in exact proportion with physical inequality – a distinction which sufficiently determines what we ought to think of that form of inequality which prevails among all civilized peoples; for it is manifestly contrary to the law of nature, however defined, that a child should govern an old man, that an imbecile should lead a wise man, and that a handful of people should gorge themselves with superfluities while the hungry multitude goes in want of necessities.[34]

ROUSSEAU'S NOTES

(A) Herodotus tells us that after the murder of the false Smerdis, when the seven liberators of Persia met to deliberate on the form of government they would give the state, Otanes came out strongly for a republic, an opinion all the more extraordinary in the mouth of a satrap in that, besides the claims he might himself have to the empire, grandees as a rule fear more than death a form of government which forces them to respect men. Otanes, one can well believe, was not heeded, and seeing that they were going on to elect a monarch, he who wished neither to obey nor to command, yielded freely to other contenders his right to the crown, and asked as his only compensation freedom and independence for himself and his posterity – which was granted him. If Herodotus did not inform us of the limitation which was placed on this privilege, one would necessarily have to assume it, otherwise Otanes, recognizing no kind of law and answerable to no one, would have been all-powerful in the state and more powerful than the king himself. But it is hardly likely that a man capable of contenting himself in such a case with such a privilege, was capable of abusing it. In fact, there is no sign that this right was ever the cause of the least trouble in the kingdom, either on the part of the wise Otanes himself or any of his descendants.

(B) From the outset, I lean with confidence on one of those authorities[1] who are respected by philosophers because they speak from a solid and sublime reason which philosophers alone know how to discover and to recognize:

'However much it is to our interest to know ourselves, I wonder if we do not know better everything which is not ourselves. Supplied by nature with organs designed uniquely for our preservation, we use them only in order to receive external impressions; we seek only to reach beyond ourselves, and exist outside ourselves; too much concerned to multiply the functions of our senses and to augment the outward extent of our being, we seldom make use of that inward sense which reduces us to our true dimensions, and separates us from all that is not part of us. However, it is this sense that we must use if we wish to know ourselves; it is the only one by which we can judge ourselves.

But how can this sense be brought into action and given its full range? How can we purge our soul, in which it resides, of all the illusions of our mind? We have lost the habit of using it; it has remained unexercised amidst the tumult of our corporael sensations, dried out by the fires of our passions; the heart, the mind, the senses – all have worked against it' (Buffon), *Histoire naturelle*, vol. IV, p. 151).[2]

(C) The changes which long practice of walking on two feet could have produced in the conformation of man, the similarities one still observes between man's arms and the front legs of quadrupeds, and the inferences drawn from their way of walking, have given rise to doubts about the way which must have been the most natural for us. Every child begins by walking on all fours and needs our example and our lessons to learn how to stand upright. There are even savage nations, such as the Hottentots who, being very neglectful of their children, let them walk on their hands for so long that they have difficulty in correcting their posture later; the children of the Caribs in the West Indies do the same. There are various instances of quadruped men; and I could quote among others the case of the child discovered in 1344, near Hesse, who had been nursed by wolves, and who said afterwards at the Court of Prince Henry that if the choice depended on him alone, he would prefer to go back to the wolves than to live among human beings. He had so completely acquired the habit of walking like those animals that it was necessary to attach pieces of wood to him to force him to stand erect and keep his balance on two feet. The same is true of the child found in 1694 in the forests of Lithuania, who had lived among bears. He gave no sign of reason, says M. de Condillac;[3] he walked on all fours, he spoke no language, and uttered sounds which in no way resembled those of a man. The little savage of Hanover who was taken several years ago to the English Court had all the trouble in the world to discipline himself to walk on two feet, and in 1719 two other savages were found in the Pyrenees who ran about the mountains in the manner of quadrupeds.[4] As for the objection that might be raised that this means depriving man of the use of his hands to which we owe so many advantages, I would answer that besides the example of monkeys, showing that hands can very well be employed in both manners, this proves only that man can put his limbs to more useful ends than those of nature, not that nature has destined man to walk differently from the way she teaches him. But there are, it seems to me, far better reasons to be invoked for saying that man is a biped. First, even if we are shown that he could have been formed originally otherwise than as we see him now and yet have become finally what he is, that would not be enough to justify the conclusion that this actually happened: for after having demonstrated the possibility of such mutations, it would still be necessary, before accepting them, to show at least their probability. Moreover, if the arms of men were apparently able to serve in case of need as legs, that is only one observation favourable to this hypothesis, against a great number which are opposed to it. The chief of these are: (a) that the way in which a man's head is attached to his body, instead of directing his eyes horizontally like those of all other animals, and as he has himself when he walks erect, would have kept him in walking on all fours with his eyes fixed on the ground, a situation very little favourable to the preservation of the individual; (b) that the tail he does not have, and of which he has no need in walking on two feet, is useful to quadrupeds, and none of them is deprived of one; (c) that the breast of a woman, very well placed for a biped who holds her child in her arms, would be so ill placed for a quadruped that none has it so situated; (d) that the height of the human hindquarters is excessive in proportion to the forelegs, so that walking on all fours means crawling on our knees, and the whole would have been an animal ill-proportioned and walking uncomfortably; (e) that if he had set his foot down flat as well as his hand, he would have had one less articulation in his back leg than the other animals, viz. the one which joins the canon bone to the tibia; (f) that in putting down only the toe of his foot, as he would undoubtedly have been constrained to do, the tarsus, without speaking of the several bones which compose it, would appear to be too big to take the place of the canon bone, and its articulations with the metatarsus and the tibia too close to give the human leg in this position the same flexibility as the legs of quadrupeds. The example of infants, being taken at an age when the natural forces are not yet developed nor the limbs strengthened proves nothing at all, and I could as well say that dogs are not destined to walk on the grounds that they only crawl several weeks after their birth. Particular facts have very little force against the universal practice of all men, even of peoples that, having had no communication with others, could not have imitated others. A child abandoned in the forest before it has learned to walk, and suckled by some beast, will have followed the example of his nurse in learning to walk like her; habit might have given him a dexterity he did not acquire from nature; and just as persons without arms succeed, by force of practice, in doing with their feet everything that we do with our hands, he will finally have succeeded in using his hands as feet.

(D) If there should be among my readers a bad enough physicist to raise objections against the hypothesis of the earth's natural fertility, I will answer him with the following passage [from Buffon's *Histoire naturelle*]:

'Since plants draw for their nourishment much more substance from air and water than they draw from the earth, it comes about that in rotting they return to the earth more than they have taken from it; besides, a forest keeps the waters of the rain by stopping evaporation. Thus in woods that had been preserved for a long time without being touched, the layer of soil that serves for vegetation would considerably increase; but as animals return less to the earth than they draw from it, and men consume enormous quantities of timber and plants for fires and other purposes, it follows that the layer of vegetative soil in an inhabited country must always diminish and become in the end like the terrain of Arabia Petraea, and so many other provinces of the Orient, which is in fact the area of most ancient habitation, where today we find only salt and sand; for the fixed salts of plants and animals remain, while all the other particles are volatilized.'*

We could add to this empirical proof from the quantity of trees and plants of every kind which cover nearly all the uninhabited islands that have been discovered in recent centuries, and from what history teaches us about the immense forests that had to be cut down all over the world as it was populated or civilized. On this subject, I shall add the following three remarks. First, if there is a form of vegetation which can compensate for the destruction of vegetable matter brought about by animals, according to M. de Buffon's argument, it is above all trees, the tops and leaves of which collect

---

* Buffon, *Histoire naturelle*, Paris, 1752, I, pp. 354-5.

and assimilate more water and vapour than do other plants. Secondly, the destruction of the soil, that is, the loss of the substance necessary to vegetation, must accelerate in proportion to the extent that the earth is more cultivated and as more industrious inhabitants consume in greater abundance all kinds of the earth's productions. My third and most important remark is that the fruits of trees provide animals with more abundant food than does any other type of vegetation; an experiment I have made myself by comparing the produce of two parcels of land equal in size and quality, the one covered with chestnut trees, the other sown with wheat.[7]

(E) Among quadrupeds the two most universal distinguishing characteristics of the voracious species are, first, the shape of the teeth and, second, the conformation of the intestines. Animals that live only on vegetation all have blunt teeth, like the horse, the ox, the sheep, the hare, while voracious animals have sharp teeth, like the cat, the dog, the wolf, the fox. As for the intestines, frugivorous animals have some, such as the colon, which are not found in voracious animals. It appears therefore that man, having teeth and intestines like the frugivorous animals, should naturally be classified in that category,[8] and it is not only anatomical observation which confirms this opinion, for the classics of antiquity are also much in its favour: 'Dicaearchus', says St Jerome, 'relates in his books on Greek antiquity, that under the reign of Saturn when the whole earth was still fertile by itself, no man ate flesh but all lived on the fruits and vegetables that grew naturally.'*
One may see from this how I leave aside many points I might exploit to support my argument. For as prey is almost the only thing carnivorous animals fight about, and as frugivorous animals live among themselves in perpetual peace, it follows that if the human race were of this latter genus, then manifestly it would have had much greater ease subsisting in the state of nature and much less need and occasion to quit it.

(F) All knowledge that requires reflection, all knowledge that is only acquired by the association of ideas and perfected only over time,

* *Against Jovinianus*. II. 13. This opinion can be further substantiated on the reports of several modern travellers. Among others, François Coréal testifies that most of the inhabitants of the Lucayes, transported by the Spaniards to the islands of Cuba, Santo Domingo and elsewhere, died as a result of eating flesh[9] [Edition of 1782].

seems altogether beyond the reach of savage man, for want of communication with his fellow man, that is to say, for want of an instrument to use for such communication, and for want of the needs which render it necessary. His knowledge and his industry are limited to leaping, running, fighting, throwing stones, climbing trees. And yet if he knows only these things, in return he knows them much better than we do, who do not have the same need of them that he has; and since such skills depend entirely on bodily practice and are not susceptible of any communication or any progress from one individual to another, the first man could have been just as good at them as his last descendants.

Travellers' reports are full of examples of the strength and the vigour of men in barbarous and savage nations; they praise hardly less their dexterity and their nimbleness; and as eyes are all that is needed to observe these things, there is no reason why we should not believe the testimony of eyewitnesses, of which I draw at random several examples from the first books that come to hand:

'The Hottentots', says Kolben,[10] 'understand fishing better than the Europeans of the Cape. Their skill is the same with the net, the hook and the barb, in coves as in rivers. They are no less adroit at catching fish by hand. They are incomparably skilful as swimmers. Their manner of swimming has something astonishing about it which is peculiar to them. They swim with the body[11] upright and their hands stretched out of the water, so they look as if they are walking on land. In the roughest seas, when the waves form so many mountains around them, they somehow dance on the crest of the waves, rising and falling like a piece of cork.'*

'The Hottentots', the same author says again, 'have a surprising dexterity at hunting, and their fleetness of foot surpasses the imagination.' He is surprised that they do not more often put their agility to bad use, which nevertheless does sometimes happen, as one can tell from an example he gives: 'A Dutch sailor disembarking at the Cape', he writes, 'employed a Hottentot to follow him to the town with a sack of tobacco weighing about twenty pounds. When they were some distance from the crew, the Hottentot asked the sailor if he knew how to run. "Run!" answered the Dutchman, "Yes, very

---

* *Histoire générale des voyages*, Paris, 1748, vol. V, pp. 155–6.

well." "We shall see," replied the African, and running away with the tobacco, he disappeared almost at once. The sailor, bewildered by such marvellous speed, did not think of chasing him, and never saw again either his tobacco or his porter.

'They have such alert vision and a hand so certain that Europeans cannot approach them. At a hundred paces they will hit a target the size of a small coin with a stone, and, what is even more astonishing is that instead of fixing their eyes on the mark as we do, they make continual movements and contortions. It seems that their stone is carried by an invisible hand.'

Father du Tertre[12] reports of the savages of the West Indies much the same things that I have just quoted about the Hottentots of the Cape of Good Hope. He praises above all their precision in shooting with their arrows at birds on the wing or fish in the water, which they catch afterwards by diving. The savages of North America are no less celebrated for their strength and their dexterity; and here is an example which allows us to judge that of the Indians of South America:

In the year 1746, an Indian of Buenos Aires, having been sentenced to the galleys of Cadiz, proposed to the Governor that he should redeem his liberty by risking his life at a public festival. He promised that he would attack alone the fiercest bull with no other weapon in his hand but a rope; that he would ground the bull, that he would seize it with his rope by whatever part he was told, that he would saddle it, bridle it, mount it, and that he would fight thus mounted two other of the angriest bulls to be let out of the Torillo; and that he would kill them, one after the other, the instant he was commanded to do so, without the help of anyone. His wish was granted. The Indian kept his word, and he succeeded in everything he had promised; as for the way he performed, and for all the details of the fight, one may consult the first volume, in $-12°$ of M. Gautier's[13] *Observations sur l'histoire naturelle*, page 262, from which these facts are taken.

(G) 'The duration of the life of horses,' says M. de Buffon,* 'as with all other species of animals, is proportionate to the length of time of growth. Man, who takes fourteen years to grow, can live for six or seven times as long, that is, to ninety or a hundred years. The

---

* *Histoire naturelle du cheval*, Paris, 1750, vol. IV, pp. 226–7.

horse, whose growth is completed in four years, can live six or seven times as long, that is, to twenty-five or thirty years. Examples which might be at variance with this rule are so rare that they ought not to be regarded as exceptions from which conclusions could be derived; and just as heavy horses reach their full growth in less time than light horses, so they live less time and are old at the age of fifteen years.'[14]

(H) I believe I see between carnivorous and frugivorous animals another difference which is even more general than the one I discussed in Note E, since this one extends also to birds. The difference consists in the number of young, which never exceeds two in each litter among the herbivorous, but ordinarily goes beyond that number among voracious animals. It is easy to learn nature's intentions in this regard from the number of teats, which is only two for each female in the first species, the mare, the cow, the goat, the doe, the ewe, etc., and which is always six or eight in the other females, such as the bitch, the cat, the wolf, the tigress, etc. The hen, the goose, the duck, which are all voracious birds, as are the eagle, the hawk, the owl, also lay and hatch a large number of eggs, something that never happens in the case of the pigeon, the turtle-dove or other birds which eat absolutely nothing but seeds, and hardly ever lay and hatch more than two eggs at a time. The reason that can be given for this difference is that animals which eat only herbs and plants, lingering almost all day at pasture and having to spend a great deal of time feeding themselves, would not be adequate to the nursing of several young ones, whereas voracious animals, taking their meals almost in an instant, can more readily and more frequently pass between their young and the hunt, and make up for the waste of such a large quantity of milk. On all this there are many particular observations and reflections to be made, but this is not the place for them, and it is enough for me to have shown in this section the most general system of nature, a system which provides a further reason for taking man out of the class of carnivorous animals and putting him among the frugivorous species.

(I) A celebrated author,* adding up the good and the bad aspects

---

*Maupertuis.

of human life and comparing the two totals, concluded that the latter greatly surpassed the former, that all in all life was a rather wretched gift to man.[15] His conclusion does not surprise me; he based all his reasoning on the constitution of civilized man. If he had gone back to natural man, we may be sure that he would have come up with very different results; he would have noticed that man has hardly had any evils except those he has given himself, and that nature would be exonerated. It is not without difficulty that we have succeeded in making ourselves so unhappy. When we consider, on the one hand, the enormous achievements of man, so many sciences developed, so many arts invented, so many forces utilized, chasms filled, mountains razed, rocks broken, rivers made navigable, land cleared, lakes carved out, marshes drained, enormous buildings erected on land, the sea covered with ships and sailors; and when, on the other hand, we search with a little meditation for the real advantages that have come out of all this for the happiness of the human race, we cannot fail to be struck by the astonishing disproportion which exists between these things, nor fail to deplore man's blindness, which in order to nourish his foolish pride and I know not what vain self-admiration, makes him run ardently after all the miseries of which he is susceptible, and which a beneficent nature had taken care to keep from him.

Men are wicked; melancholy and constant experience removes any need for proof. Yet man is naturally good;[16] I believe I have demonstrated it. What then can have corrupted him to this point, if not the changes that have come about in his constitution, the progress he has made, and the knowledge he has acquired? Admire human society as you will, it is nonetheless true that it necessarily leads men to hate each other in proportion to the extent that their interests conflict, and to pretend to render each other services while actually doing each other every imaginable harm. What is one to think of a system in which the reason of each private person dictates to him maxims contrary to the maxims which the public reason preaches to the body of society, a system in which each finds his profit in the misfortunes of others? There is perhaps not one man of property whose death is not secretly desired by his greedy heirs and often indeed by his own children; no ship at sea whose wreck would not be good news for some merchant; no business house that some dishonest debtor would not wish to see burn down with all its papers in it; no nation that does not rejoice in the disasters of its neighbours. It is thus that we each find our profit at the expense of our fellows; and one man's loss is nearly always the good fortune of another. But what is even more dangerous is that public calamities are looked for and hoped for by a multitude of individuals. Some wish for diseases, others death, others war, others famine; I have seen abominable men weep with sorrow at the prospect of a good harvest; and the great deadly Fire of London which cost the lives and possessions of so many ill-fated victims made the fortunes perhaps of more than a thousand persons. I know that Montaigne blames the Athenian Demades for having punished a worker who profited from the death of citizens by selling coffins at a very high price, but from the reason that Montaigne gives, namely that everybody ought to have been punished, it is obvious that he confirms my reasoning. Let us therefore look underneath all our fanciful displays of benevolence at what goes on at the bottom of our hearts and let us consider what must be the state of affairs where all men are forced simultaneously to caress and to destroy each other, and where duty makes them enemies and interest makes them rogues. If I am answered by the assertion that society is so constituted that each man gains by serving others, I shall reply that that would be all very well but for the fact that he would gain even more by harming them. There is no profit so legitimate that it cannot be exceeded by what can be made illegitimately and an injury done to a neighbour is always more lucrative than any service. The only problem that remains is that of finding ways of assuring one's impunity; and this is the end for which the powerful use all their strength and the weak use all their cunning.

Savage man, when he has eaten, is at peace with the whole of nature and the friend of all his fellow-men. Is it a matter of disputing his meal? He will never come to blows over it without first comparing the difficulty of winning with that of finding his sustenance elsewhere, and as pride does not enter into the fight, it is ended by a few fisticuffs; the victor eats, the vanquished goes off to seek better luck elsewhere, and all is pacified. But in the case of man in society, these are very different matters: in the first place it is a question of providing what is necessary, next what is superfluous, then afterwards come luxuries, then immense riches, then subjects, then slaves; man in society does not have a moment of respite. What is the more singular is that the less natural and urgent the needs, the more the desires increase, and what is worse, so does the power to satisfy them; so that after a long experience of prosperity, and after having consumed many treasures and distressed many men, my hero will end by cutting every throat until he is the sole master of the universe. Such is the moral portrait, if not of human life, at least of the secret ambitions of the heart of every civilized man.[17]

Compare without prejudice the condition of the civilized man with that of the savage, and investigate, if you can, how, aside from his wickedness, his needs and his miseries, the civilized man has opened new doors to suffering and to death. If you consider the anguish of mind which consumes us, the violent passions which exhaust and grieve us, the excessive labours with which the poor are overburdened, and the even more dangerous laxity to which the rich abandon themselves, so that the former die of their needs while the latter of their excesses; if you think of the monstrous mixtures they eat, their pernicious seasonings, their corrupt foods and adulterated drugs; the cheating of those who sell such things and the mistakes of those who administer them, of the poison in the vessels used for cooking;[18] if you take note of the epidemic diseases engendered by the bad air where multitudes of men are gathered together, take note also of those occasioned by the delicacy of our way of life, by our moving between the interiors of houses and the open air, by the use of clothes put on or taken off with too little precaution, and all the cares that our excessive sensuality has turned into necessary habits and of which the neglect or deprivation then costs us our life or our health; if you take also into consideration fires which consume and earthquakes which overthrow whole cities, killing their inhabitants by thousands; in a word, if you add up the dangers that all these causes continually put together over our heads, you will see how dearly nature makes us pay for the contempt we have shown for her lessons.

I shall not repeat here what I have said elsewhere on the subject of war,* but I wish that educated men desired or dared for once to tell the public the details of the horrors for which contractors of military supplies and hospitals are responsible. We should see their none too secret manoeuvres make the most brilliant armies melt into

---

* *L'état de guerre*, OC, III, pp. 601–16 [BVN, MS.R 32].

less than nothing and cause more soldiers to perish than are cut down by the enemy's steel. It is a reckoning no less astonishing to count the men the sea swallows up every year, whether by hunger, or scurvy, or pirates, or fire or shipwreck. We must attribute to the institution of property, and hence to society, murders, poisonings, highway robberies, and indeed the punishments of those crimes, punishments which are necessary for the prevention of greater evils, but which, for every murder of one man cost the lives of two or more men and so actually double the loss to the human species. How many shameful methods there are to prevent the birth of man and deceive nature; whether by those brutish and depraved tastes which insult her most charming work, tastes that neither savages nor animals have ever known, and which are born in civilized countries only from corrupt imaginations;[19] whether by secret abortions, worthy fruits of debauchery and vicious honour; whether by the exposure and murder of a multitude of infants, victims of the poverty of their parents or the barbarous shame of their mothers,[20] finally, by the mutilation of those unfortunates, in whom a part of their existence and all their posterity are sacrificed for the sake of some worthless songs, or worse still sacrificed to the brutal jealousy of a few men; a mutilation which, in this last case, doubly outrages nature, both in the treatment received by the victims and the use to which they are destined.*

* But are there not cases, a thousand times more frequent and dangerous where paternal rights openly offend humanity? How many talents are suppressed and inclinations forced by the unwise constraint of fathers! How many men would be distinguished in the right situation but die unhappy and dishonoured in another situation for which they have no taste! How many happy but unequal marriages have been broken or disturbed, and how many chaste wives dishonoured by an arrangement of circumstances which is always contrary to nature! How many other bizarre unions are formed by interest and disavowed by love and reason! How many even honest and virtuous spouses torment each other just because they are ill-matched! How many young and unhappy victims of their parents' greed plunge themselves into vice or spend their sad days weeping, groaning in unbreakable ties which the heart rejects and which gold alone has formed! Happy sometimes are those whose courage and even whose virtue delivers them from life before a barbarous violence forces them into crime or despair. Forgive me, father and mother forever lamenting; it is with regret that I embitter your sufferings; but it may serve as an eternal and terrible example to anyone who dares, in the very name of nature, to violate the most sacred of its rights!

If I have spoken only of those ill-formed marriages which are the work of our civilization, is it to be thought that those over which love and sympathy have presided are without their disadvantages? [Edition of 1782].

What would happen if I undertook to show the human race attacked at its very source,[21] and even in the most sacred of all bonds, where one no longer dares to listen to nature until after consulting one's purse, and where, with disorder in society confusing virtues and vices, continence becomes a criminal precaution and the refusal to give life to one's fellow-being[22] an act of humanity? But without stripping the veil which covers so many horrors, let us be content to point out the evil for which others must supply the remedy.

When one adds to all this the numbers of unhealthy trades which shorten lives or ruin men's physique – trades such as labouring in mines, various preparations of metals, minerals and especially lead, copper, mercury, cobalt, arsenic, realgar,[23] together with those other dangerous trades which daily cost the lives of numerous workers, some roofers, others carpenters, or masons, or labourers in quarries – if one adds together, I say, all these negative factors, then one can see in the establishment and improvement of societies the explanation of that diminution of the species which has been observed by more than one philosopher.

Luxury, impossible to prevent among men who are greedy for their own comforts and for consideration from others, soon completes the damage that societies begin, and on the pretext of keeping alive the poor, a pretext of which there is no need, luxury impoverishes everyone else, and sooner or later depopulates the state.

Luxury is a remedy much worse than the evil it claims to cure,[24] or rather it is itself the worst of evils in any state, however small or great that state may be; and in order to feed the crowds of lackeys and wretches it creates, luxury crushes and ruins the farmer and the townsman; it resembles those burning winds of the South which, by covering the grass and greenery with devouring insects, rob useful animals of their subsistence and bring famine and death to every place they touch.

From society and the luxury which society engenders are born the liberal and mechanical arts, commerce, literature and all those useless things which, in making industry flourish, enrich and destroy states. The reason for this deterioration is very simple. It is easy to see that agriculture by its nature is bound to be the least lucrative of all the arts, because its products, being the most indispensable for all men, must fetch a price in proportion to the reach of the poorest.

From the same principle we can derive this rule: that in general the arts are lucrative in inverse proportion to their utility, and the most necessary are bound to become in the end the most neglected. From this we see what must be considered the true advantages of industry and the real outcome which results from its progress.

Such are the palpable causes of all the miseries into which opulence plunges the most admired nations. As industry and the arts extend and flourish, the despised farmer, burdened with the taxes which are necessary for the maintenance of luxury, and condemned to divide his life between labour and hunger, abandons his fields to seek in the towns the bread he ought to be taking there. The more capital cities excite admiration in the stupid eyes of the people, the more we shall have to weep at the sight of the countryside abandoned, the land fallow, and the highways flooded with unhappy citizens turned beggars or thieves, destined to end their misery one day on the rack or on a dungheap. It is thus that the state, enriching itself on the one hand, enfeebles and depopulates itself on the other, and thus that the most powerful monarchies, after many efforts to make themselves opulent and empty, end up becoming the prey of poor nations which succumb to the fatal temptation to invade them, only to enrich and enfeeble themselves in their turn, until they too are invaded and destroyed by others.

Let someone deign to explain to us for once what could have produced those hordes of barbarians who for so many centuries swamped Europe, Asia and Africa. Was it to the industry of their arts, to the wisdom of their laws, and the excellence of their civil constitutions that they owed that prodigious population? Let our scholars kindly tell us why, far from multiplying to that point, these ferocious and brutish men, without science, without restraint, without education, did not murder each other at every instant in fighting over their food or game? Let our scholars explain how those wretched men had even the audacity to look in the face such clever men as we were, with such fine military discipline, such fine codes and such wise laws; and finally, explain why after society was improved in the countries of the North, and after such trouble had been taken to teach men their mutual duties and the art of living agreeably and peacefully together, nothing more is seen to come from them resembling those multitudes of men that were formerly produced.

I am afraid that someone may finally decide to say in reply to me that all those great things – arts, sciences and laws – have been very wisely invented by men as a salutary plague to prevent the excessive multiplication of the species, for fear that this world, which is destined for us, might finally become too small for its inhabitants.

What then?[25] Must we destroy societies, annihilate *meum* and *teum* and return to live in the forests with the bears? A conclusion in the style of my adversaries, which I would sooner forestall than permit them to disgrace themselves by drawing. Oh you, to whom the heavenly voice has not made itself heard, and who recognize no other destiny for your species than to complete this brief life in peace; you who can leave your fatal acquisitions, your troubled spirits, your corrupt hearts and your frenzied desires in the midst of cities, reclaim – since it is up to you to do so – your ancient and first innocence; go into the woods and loose the sight and memory of the crimes of your contemporaries, and have no fear of debasing your species in renouncing its enlightenment in order to renounce its vices. As for men like me, whose passions have destroyed their original simplicity for ever, who can no longer nourish themselves on herbs and nuts, nor do without laws and rulers; those whose forefathers were honoured with supernatural lessons, those who can see in the intention of giving from the beginning a morality to human actions which they would not otherwise have acquired for a long time, the reason for a precept indifferent in itself and inexplicable in any other system; those, in a word, who are convinced that the divine voice called the whole human race to the enlightenment and happiness of celestial intelligences; all those will endeavour, by the exercise of virtues which they commit themselves to practise while learning to understand them, to deserve the eternal prize they ought to expect for them; they will respect the sacred bonds of the societies of which they are members; they will love their fellow-men and serve them with all their strength; they will scrupulously obey the laws and the men who are the authors and ministers of the laws; they will honour above all the good and wise princes who know how to prevent, cure and relieve that mass of abuses and evils which are always ready to overwhelm us; they will animate the zeal of those worthy rulers, in showing them without fear or flattery the greatness of their task and the rigour of their duty, but they will nonetheless despise a constitution that can be maintained only with the help of numerous estimable persons who are desired more often than they are found, a constitution from which, in spite of their cares, there will always arise more real calamities than seeming advantages.

(J) Among the men we know, either through our own acquaintance, or through historians or travellers, some are black, others white, others red; some have long hair, others have only woolly curls, some are almost covered in hair, others have not even a beard. There have been, and perhaps still are, peoples of gigantic height, and leaving aside the fable of the pygmies, which may well be only an exaggeration, we know that the Laplanders and especially the Greenlanders, are very much below the average height of man. It is even claimed that there are entire peoples with tails like quadrupeds, and without giving blind faith to the reports of Herodotus and Ctesias, one can at least take from them this very probable opinion – if one could have made sound observations in ancient times when various peoples' ways of life which differed among themselves to a greater extent than do those of peoples today, one would have observed in the shapes and structure of the body much more striking varieties. All these facts, of which it is easy to supply incontestable proofs, could only surprise those who are accustomed to looking simply at the objects which surround them, and who are ignorant of the powerful effects of the diversity of environments, of the air, of foods, of the style of living, of habits in general, and above all, the astonishing effects of the same causes when they act continually over a long series of generations. Today when trade, travel and conquests bring various peoples closer together, and when their ways of living become constantly more alike as a result of frequent communication, one notices that certain national differences have diminished, and everyone can see, for example, that the French of today have no longer those tall, blond, pale bodies described by the Latin historians, although time, together with the intermingling of Franks and Normans, themselves pale and blond, should have restored what frequentation with the Romans may have done to reduce the influence of the climate over the natural constitution and the complexion of the inhabitants. All these observations on the variety which a thousand causes can produce and in fact have produced in the human species, prompt me to doubt whether those very different animals resembling man and taken by travellers without much scrutiny to be beasts, either because of a few differences they observed in external conformation, or simply because the animal did not speak, were not in fact real savage men, whose race, dispersed since antiquity in the forests, with no opportunity to develop any of its potential faculties, had not acquired any measure of perfection, and was still found in the primitive state of nature.[26] Let me give an example of what I have in mind:

'In the Kingdom of the Congo', says the translator of the *Histoire des voyages*,* 'one finds many of those large animals which are called *orang-outangs*[27] in the East Indies, and which stand half-way between the human species and baboons.[28] Andrew Battel[29] relates that in the forests of Mayomba in the Kingdom of Loango, one sees two sorts of monsters, of which the larger are called *pongos* and the smaller *enjocos*. The former bear an exact resemblance to man, but they are much heavier and they are very tall. With a human face, they have the eyes deep set. Their hands, their cheeks and their ears are without hair, except for the eyebrows, which are very long. Although the rest of the body is rather hairy, the hair itself is not very thick and its colour is brown. Finally, the only feature which distinguishes them from men is the leg, which has no calf. They walk upright, with a hand on the hair of another's neck; their retreat is in the forest; they sleep in the trees, and there they make a sort of roof which shelters them from the rain. Their food consists of fruits or wild nuts. They never eat flesh. The custom of Negroes[30] who travel in the forests is to light fires during the night. They notice that in the mornings after they have left the pongos take their places around the fire, and do not go away until the fire dies out; for with all their dexterity, they do not have enough sense to keep the fire going by putting on more wood.

'They sometimes walk in bands and kill Negroes who cross the forests. They even fall on elephants who come to graze in the places where they live, and they annoy them so much with blows from their fists or sticks that they force them to go away screaming. Pongos can never be caught alive because they are so violent that ten men would not be enough to hold one; but the Africans take many young

---

* *Histoire générale des voyages*,[31] Paris, 1748, Book XIII, pp. 87–9.

ones after having killed the mother, to whose body the young cling fiercely. When one of these animals dies, the others cover the corpse with a pile of branches or leaves.' Samuel Purchas adds that in the conversation he had with Andrew Battel, he learned from him how a pongo abducted a little Negro, who passed a whole month in the society of these animals, for they do no harm to men they surprise, at least so long as those men pay no attention to them, as the little Negro had done. Battel did not describe the second species of monster.

'Dapper[32] confirms that the Kingdom of the Congo is full of these animals which bear in the East Indies the name of "orang-outangs". that is to say "inhabitants of the woods" and which the Africans call "quojas-morros". This beast, he says, is so like a man that it has given several travellers the idea that it could be the issue of a woman and an ape, a chimera that even the Negroes reject. One of these animals was transported from the Congo to Holland and presented to the Prince of Orange, Frederick-Henry. It was as tall as a child of three years and moderately fat, but square and well-proportioned, very agile and lively, the legs fleshy and robust, the whole front of the body hairless but the back covered with black hair. At first glance its face resembled that of a man, but its nose was flat and curved; the ears were also those of the human species; its breast – for it was a female – was plump, its navel deep, its shoulders very well set, its hands divided into fingers and thumbs, its calves and its heels thick and fleshy. It often walked upright on its legs; it was able to lift and carry fairly heavy burdens. When it wanted to drink it took the lid off the pot with one hand, and held the base with the other. Afterwards it wiped its lips politely. It lay down to sleep, its head on a pillow, covering itself with so much grace that one would take it for a man in bed. The Negroes tell strange stories about this animal. They not only declare that it violates women and girls, but that it dares to attack armed men. In a word, there is much to suggest that it is the Satyr of the Ancients. Merolla[33] perhaps speaks of just these when he records that the Africans hunting sometimes catch savage men and women.'

In the third[34] volume of this same *Histoire des voyages*, there is more about these species of anthropomorphic animals under the names of *beggos* and *mandrills*. But to confine ourselves to the reports just quoted, we find in the descriptions of these supposed monsters striking conformities with the human species and fewer differences from men than those between one man and another. One cannot see in these passages why the author refuses to give the animals in question the name of savage men, but one may readily guess that it is because of the stupidity of the creatures, and also because they did not talk – a poor reason for those who know that although the organ of speech is natural to man, speech itself is not natural to him, and who know to what level self-improvement has elevated the civilized man above his original state. The small measure of coherence these descriptions contain enables us to judge how badly the animals were observed and with what prejudices they were judged. For example, they are classified as monsters and yet it is admitted that they reproduced themselves. In one place Battel says the pongos kill Negroes who cross the forests; in another, Purchas says they do them no harm even when they surprise them, at least so long as the Negroes make no effort to pay attention to them. The pongos gather around fires lit by Negroes when the latter go away, and go away in turn when the fire dies out; there is the fact – now let us read the comment of the observer: *'for with all their dexterity, they do not have enough sense to keep the fire going by putting on more wood.'* I wish I could imagine how Battel, or Purchas[35] his editor, could have known that the departure of the pongos was an outcome of their stupidity rather than their will. In a climate like that of Loango, fire is not a thing very necessary for animals, and if the Negroes light them, it is less to protect themselves against the cold than to frighten off wild beasts. It is therefore very easy to understand that after having enjoyed the flames for a while and being thoroughly warmed, the pongos become bored with staying always in the same place, and go off to seek their food, which requires all the more time since they do not eat flesh. Besides, we know that the majority of animals, not excepting man, are naturally lazy, and they resist cares of any kind that are not an absolute necessity. Finally, it seems very odd that the pongos, whose dexterity and strength is acknowledged, who know how to bury their dead and who build themselves roofs of branches, should not know how to push logs on a fire. I can remember seeing a monkey perform this very manoeuvre that pongos are said to be unable to perform; it is true that my thoughts not being at that time directed to this question, I committed the fault for which I reproach the travellers: I failed to examine whether the monkey's intention was in fact to maintain the fire or, as I believe, to imitate the action of a man. But whatever is the case, it is well proven that the ape is not a variety of man, not only because he is deprived of the faculty of speech, but above all because we are sure that his species does not have the faculty of self-improvement which is the specific characteristic of the human race. Experiments do not appear to have been made on the pongo and the orang-outang with enough precision for us to draw the same conclusion in their case. There would, however, be a method by which, if the orang-outang and others were of the human species, the crudest observers could assure themselves of it even by demonstration; but since a single generation would not suffice for this experiment, it must be considered impracticable, because it would be necessary for what is only an hypothesis to be already proved true before the experiment that was to prove it true could be tried innocently.

Precipitate judgements which are not the fruit of an enlightened reason are apt to be extravagant. Our travellers do not hesitate to treat as beasts under the names of pongos, mandrills and orang-outangs the same creatures that the ancients, under the names of satyrs, fawns and nymphs, made into divinities. Perhaps after more exact research, we shall find that they are men.* In the meantime, it seems to me that there is as much reason to listen to Merolla, an educated monk and eyewitness who, for all his unworldliness, was nevertheless a man of intelligence, as there is reason to listen to the merchant Battel, or Dapper or Purchas and the other compilers of books.

What verdict, is it thought, would such observers have given in the case of the child found in 1694, about whom I have spoken already, the child who gave no sign of reason, walked on all fours, had no language, and made noises which did not in any way resemble human sounds? It was a long time, according to the philosopher† who gave me these facts, before the child could pronounce a few words, and he did that in a barbarous fashion. As soon as he was able to speak, he was interrogated about his first condition, but he could remember it no more than we can remember what happened to us in the cradle. If, unluckily for him, this child had fallen into the hands of our travellers, we cannot doubt that after noting his silence and stupidity,

* We shall find that they are neither beasts nor gods, but men [Edition of 1782].
† Condillac.

they would have taken it upon themselves to send him back into the forest or shut him up in a menagerie, after which they would have spoken learnedly about him in their splendid narratives as a very curious beast somewhat resembling a man.

In the two or three centuries since the inhabitants of Europe have been flooding into other parts of the world, endlessly publishing new collections of voyages and travel, I am persuaded that we have come to know no other men except Europeans; moreover it appears from the ridiculous prejudices, which have not died out even among men of letters, that every author produces under the pompous name of the study of man nothing much more than a study of the men of his own country. Individuals go here and there in vain; it seems that philosophy does not travel and that the philosophy of one nation proves little suited to another. The cause of this is obvious, at least in the case of distant countries. There are hardly more than four sorts of men who make long-distance voyages: sailors, merchants, soldiers and missionaries. Now it can hardly be expected that the first three classes should yield good observers, and as for the fourth, taken up with the sublime vocation to which they have been called, even if they are not subject to the same prejudices of rank as are all the others, one must believe that they would not lend themselves willingly to researches that would look like pure curiosity and distract their attention from the more important labours to which they have committed themselves. Besides, to preach the Gospel usefully, it is only necessary to have zeal and God supplies the rest; but to study man it is necessary to have talents that God is not obliged to give to anyone, and which are not always possessed by saints. One does not open a book of voyages without finding descriptions of characters and customs, but one is altogether amazed to find that these authors who describe so many things tell us only what all of them knew already, and have only learned how to see at the other end of the world what they would to have been able to see without leaving their own street, and that the real features which distinguish nations, and which strike eyes made to see them, have almost always escaped their notice. Hence that fine adage of ethics, so often repeated by the philosophistical throng:[36] that men are everywhere the same, and since they all have the same passions and the same vices, it is pretty useless to seek to characterize different peoples – which is as reasonable as saying that one cannot distinguish Pierre from Jacques, since they both have a nose, a mouth and eyes.

Shall we never see reborn those happy times when the people did not meddle in philosophy, but when a Plato, a Thales, a Pythagoras, impelled by an ardent desire for knowledge, undertook the most extensive voyages solely to instruct themselves, and travelled far in order to shake off the yoke of national prejudices, to learn to study men by their resemblances and their differences, and to acquire a universal knowledge which was not that of one century or one country exclusively, but being that of all times and all places, was, so to speak, the universal science of the wise?

We admire the magnificence of several men whose curiosity has made them undertake, or have undertaken, at great expense expeditions to the East with scholars and artists, to make drawings of ruins there or to decipher and copy inscriptions; but I find it hard to imagine why in a century which prides itself on its fine sciences, we do not find two well-matched men, rich, the one in money, the other in genius, both loving glory and aspiring to immortality, two men who would sacrifice, in the one case twenty thousand crowns of his property, in the other, ten years of his life, so as to make a glorious voyage round the world in order to study, not eternally plants and stones, but for once men and customs; and who, after all the centuries that have been spent measuring and appraising the house, should finally decide that they would like to have knowledge of the inhabitants.

The Academicians who have travelled to the northern parts of Europe and the southern parts of America have gone to visit those places rather as geometers than as philosophers. However, since some have been both, we cannot regard as entirely unknown the regions seen and described by such as La Condamine[37] and Maupertuis.[38] The jeweller Chardin,[39] who travelled like Plato, has left nothing more to be said about Persia; China seems to have been well observed by the Jesuits. Kaempfer[40] gives a tolerable idea of the little he saw of Japan. Apart from these narratives, we know nothing of the peoples of the East Indies, visited only by Europeans eager to fill their purses rather than their minds. The whole of Africa with its numerous inhabitants, as remarkable in character as in colour, is yet to be studied. The entire world is covered with peoples of whom we know only the names, and yet we amuse ourselves judging the human race!

Suppose a Montesquieu, a Buffon, a Diderot, a Duclos, a D'Alembert, a Condillac and other men of that stamp were to travel to instruct their compatriots, observing and describing as only they know how, Turkey, Egypt, Barbary, the Empire of Morocco, Guinea, the land of the Kaffirs, the interior and the East coast of Africa, the Malabars, Mogul, the banks of the Ganges, the kingdoms of Siam, Pegu and Ava. China, Tartary and above all Japan, and then in the other hemisphere, Mexico, Peru, Chile, and Magellan lands, not forgetting the Patagonias, true and false; Tucamen, Paraguay if possible, Brazil; finally the Caribbean islands, Florida and all the savage countries – the most important voyage of all, and the one that would have to be undertaken with the greatest possible care. Suppose that these new Hercules, on their return from these memorable journeys, then wrote at leisure the natural, moral and political history of what they had seen, we ourselves would see a new world spring from under their pens, and we should learn thereby to know our own world. If such observers as these were to assert of an animal that it is a man and of another animal that it is a beast, then I say we must believe them; but it would be excessively naïve to accept the authority of uncultured travellers about whom one is sometimes tempted to ask the very question that they take it upon themselves to answer in the case of other animals.

(K) All this seems to me manifestly evident, and I cannot imagine where our philosophers locate the origin of all the passions they attribute to natural man. Apart from the physically necessary, which nature itself demands, all our other needs are needs only because of habit, prior to which they are not needs at all, or because of our desires, and one does not desire what one is no position to know about. From this it follows in the case of the savage man who desires only the things he knows and knows only things within his reach, or easy to acquire, that nothing ought to be so tranquil as his soul and nothing so limited as his mind.

(L) I find in Locke's *Of Civil Government** an objection[41] which seems to be too specious for me to feel free to conceal it: 'The end of conjunction between male and female', says this philosopher, 'being not

---

* *Two Treatises of Government*, Book II, chap. VII, pp. 78–80.

barely procreation but the continuation of the species, this conjunction betwixt male and female ought to last, even after procreation, so long as is necessary to the nourishment and support of young ones, who are to be sustained by those that begot them, till they be able to shift and provide for themselves. This rule, which the infinite wise Maker hath set to the works of his hands, we find the inferior creatures steadily obey. In those viviparous animals which feed on grass, the conjunction between male and female lasts no longer than the very act of copulation; because the teat of the dam being sufficient to nourish the young till it be able to feed on grass, the male only begets, but concerns not himself for the female or young, to whose sustenance he can contribute nothing. But in beasts of prey the conjunction lasts longer, because the dam, not being able well to subsist herself and nourish her numerous offspring by her own prey alone, a more laborious as well as more dangerous way of living than feeding on grass, the assistance of the male is necessary to the maintenance of their common family, if one may use that term, which cannot subsist till they are able to prey for themselves, but by the joint care of male and female. The same is to be observed in all birds (except some domestic ones where plenty of food excuses the cock from feeding and taking care of the young brood) whose young needing food in the nest, the cock and hen continue mates till the young are able to use their wings and provide for themselves.

'And therein I think lies the chief, if not the only reason, why the male and female in mankind are tied to a longer conjunction than other creatures, viz. because the female is capable of conceiving, and *de facto* is commonly with child again, and brings forth, too, a new birth long before the former is out of dependency for support on his parents' help and able to shift for himself, and has all the assistance that is due to him from his parents; whereby the father, who is bound to take care of those he hath begot, is under obligation to continue in conjugal society with the same woman longer than other creatures, whose young being able to subsist for themselves before the time of procreation returns again, the conjugal bond dissolves of itself, and they are at liberty, till Hymen at his usual anniversary season summons them again to choose their mates. Wherein one cannot but admire the wisdom of the great Creator, who having given to man foresight, and an ability to lay up for the future, as well as to supply the present necessity, hath made it necessary that the society of man and wife should be more lasting than that of male and female amongst other creatures; that so their industry might be encouraged and their interest better united, to make provision and lay up goods for their common issue, which uncertain mixture or easy and frequent dissolutions of conjugal society would mightily disturb.'

The same love of truth which has prompted me to present this objection frankly prompts me to add to it a few remarks, if not to answer it at least to clarify it:

1. In the first place I shall note that moral proofs do not have great force in the field of science and that they serve rather to justify existing facts than to establish the real existence of those facts. Now such is the kind of proof Mr Locke uses in the passage I have just quoted; for although it might be advantageous to the human race if the union of man and woman were permanent, it does not follow that it has been established thus by nature; otherwise we should have to say that nature had also instituted civil society, the arts, commerce and everything else considered useful to mankind.

2. I do not know where Mr Locke discovered that the society of male and female lasts longer among animals of prey than among those that live on grass, and that the male among them helps the female to feed the young, for we do not see that dogs, cats, bears or wolves recognize their female better than horses, rams, stags, or any other quadrupeds recognize theirs. It seems, on the contrary, that if the help of the male were necessary to the female to maintain her young, this would be true above all of species which live only on grass, because the mother requires a very long time to graze and during this interval she is forced to neglect her brood, while the prey of a female bear or wolf is devoured in an instant, and she has all the more time, without suffering hunger, to nurse her young. My argument is confirmed by an observation of the relative number of teats and young which distinguishes the carnivorous from the frugivorous species, of which I have spoken in note H. If that observation is correct and universal, the fact that a woman has only two teats and usually gives birth to only one child at a time provides one more strong reason for doubting whether the human species is naturally carnivorous. So that to reach Mr Locke's conclusion we would have to turn his reasoning upside down. There is no more substance in the

same distinction, applied to birds. For who could persuade himself that the union of male and female is more durable among the vultures and ravens than among the turtledoves? We have two species of domestic birds, the duck and the pigeon, which furnish us with examples directly contrary to the system of this author. The pigeon which feeds itself only on seeds remains united with its female, and the pair nourish their young in common. The drake, of which the voracity is well known, recognizes neither its female nor its young, and contributes in no way to their subsistence. And among hens, a species hardly less carnivorous, we do not see the cock take any trouble at all over the brood. If in other species the male shares with the female the care of feeding the young, it is because birds, which cannot fly at first and which the mother cannot nurse, are less able to do without the father's help than are quadrupeds, for whom the teat of the mother suffices, at least for a certain time.

3. There is much uncertainty about the principal fact which serves as the basis of Mr Locke's whole argument; for in order to know if it is the case, as he claims, that in the pure state of nature the woman is ordinarily pregnant again and gives birth to a new child long before the preceding child is able to fend for himself, it would be necessary to make experiments that Mr Locke has assuredly not made and which nobody is in a position to make. The continual cohabitation of husband and wife is a circumstance so conducive to a prompt renewal of pregnancy that it is difficult to believe that chance encounters or the impulse of temperament alone would produce effects as frequently in the pure state of nature as are produced in the state of conjugal society: such longer intervals between childbearing would perhaps tend to make the children more robust and might furthermore be compensated by the capacity for conception being prolonged to a greater age among women who had abused it less in their youth. As for children, there are many reasons for believing that their strength and their organs develop later among us than they did in the primitive state of which I speak. The original weakness that children inherit from the constitution of their parents, the care that is taken to wrap up and constrict all their limbs, the softness in which children are brought up, and perhaps the use of another milk than that of their mother – all this thwarts and retards in them the first progress of nature. The concentration they are obliged to

dedicate to a thousand things on which their minds are continually fixed, while no exercise is given to their bodily faculties, may further effect a considerable distortion of their growth; so that if instead of at first overburdening and tiring their minds in a thousand ways, their bodies were allowed to be exercised by the continual movements that nature seems to demand of them, one may believe that they would much sooner be able to walk, to act and fend for themselves.

4. Finally, Mr Locke proves at most that there might well be a motive for the man to stay attached to a woman while she has a child, but he proves in no way that the man must have been attached[42] to her before the birth and during the nine months of pregnancy. If a certain woman is indifferent to the man during these nine months, if indeed she becomes a stranger to him, why should he help her after the birth? Why would he help her to raise a child he does not know is his, and whose birth he has neither desired nor foreseen? Mr Locke evidently presupposes that which is in question: for it is not a matter of knowing why the man should remain attached to the woman after the birth, but why he should become attached to her after the conception. His appetite satisfied, the man has no longer any need for a particular woman, nor the woman for a particular man. The man has not the least care, nor perhaps the least idea, of the consequences of his action. One goes off in one direction, the other in another, and there is no likelihood that at the end of nine months either will remember having known the other – for that kind of memory through which one individual gives preference to another individual for the act of sexual congress requires, as I have proved in the text of this discourse, more progress – or more corruption – in human understanding than one can ascribe to the state of animality with which we are dealing here. A different woman can thus satisfy renewed desires in the man just as readily as can the woman he has already known, and a different man satisfy that woman in the same way, supposing she were to be driven by the same appetite during the state of pregnancy, which may reasonably be doubted. If in the state of nature the woman no longer feels the passion of love after the conception of the child, the obstacle to her union with the man becomes thereby even greater, since she has no longer any need either of the man who has impregnated her or of any other man. Hence there is no reason for the man to seek the same woman or for the

woman to seek the same man. Mr Locke's argument thus falls in ruins, and all the dialectics of this philosopher have not saved him from the mistake that Hobbes and others made. They had to explain a fact about the state of nature, that is, a state where men lived in isolation and where one particular man had no motive to live near another man, nor perhaps men a motive to live near other men, which is much worse; and these philosophers did not think of looking back across the centuries of society, that is to say, beyond times when men have always a reason to live close to one another, and when a particular man has often a reason to live close to a particular man or a particular woman.

(M) I shall take care not to embark on the philosophical reflections which need to be undertaken on the advantages and disadvantages of this institution of languages: I would not be allowed to attack the people's errors; and the educated are too attached to their prejudices to endure my so-called paradoxes with patience. Therefore let me quote someone who has not committed the crime of sometimes daring to take the side of reason against the opinion of the multitude: 'It would in no way diminish the happiness of mankind if, banishing the deadly and confusing multiplicity of languages, all men were to cultivate one single and uniform art – and be able to express themselves on all subjects by means of signs, movements and gestures. As things are, the condition of animals that the vulgar call beasts seems in this regard very much better than our own, for they make their feelings and thoughts understood more swiftly and perhaps more truly, without any distortion, and in this they are superior to men, especially men speaking a foreign language' (Isaac Vossius*).

(N) Plato, showing how ideas of what we call integers and their relations are necessary to the least of arts, justifiably mocks the authors of his time who claimed that Palamedes had invented numbers at the siege of Troy; as if, says that philosopher, Agamemnon could have been ignorant until that time of how many legs he had.[43] In fact, one realizes the impossibility of society and the sciences having reached the stage they had at the time of the siege of Troy without men

---

* *De Poematum cantu et viribus rythm:*, Oxford, 1673, pp. 65–6.

having had the use of numbers and arithmetic. But the necessity of having knowledge of numbers prior to the acquisition of other knowledge does not render their invention any easier to imagine; the names of numbers once known, it is easy to explain their meaning and to evoke the ideas which the names represent, but in order to invent them, it would be necessary before conceiving these same ideas, to be, so to speak, accustomed to philosophical meditations, to have applied oneself to considering entities in their pure essence and independently of all other perception, an act of abstraction which is very difficult, very metaphysical, very unnatural, and yet without which these ideas could never be carried from one species or one genus to another, nor could numbers become universal. A savage could consider separately his right leg and his left leg, or contemplate them together under the indivisible idea of a couple without ever thinking that he had two of them; for the representative idea which depicts an object for us is one thing and a numerical idea which defines an object is another. Still less could a savage have counted up to five, and even though by putting his hands together he could see that the fingers corresponded exactly, he was still far from thinking of their numerical equality. He no more knew the number of his fingers than he knew the number of the hairs on his head, and if someone, having made him understand what numbers are, then told him that he had as many toes as fingers, he would perhaps have been very surprised, in comparing them, to discover that it was true.

(O) One must not confuse pride* and self-love,† two passions very different in their nature and in their effects.[44] Self-love is a natural sentiment which prompts every animal to watch over its own conservation and which, directed in man by reason and modified by pity, produces humanity and virtue. Pride is only a relative, artificial sentiment born in society, a sentiment which prompts each individual to attach more importance to himself than to anyone else, which inspires all the injuries men do to themselves and others, and which is the true source of honour.

This being well understood, I will say that in our primitive state, in the true state of nature, pride does not exist; for with each individual

---

* *amour-propre.* † *amour de soi.*

regarding himself as the sole spectator by whom he is observed and the sole judge of his own merit, it follows that a sentiment which has its origin in comparisons he is unable to make could not possibly begin to exist in his soul. For the same reason this man could experience neither hatred nor the desire for vengeance, passions which can arise only from a belief that an offence has been received; and as it is the contempt, or the intention to hurt, and not the harm itself that constitutes an offence, men who do not know how to evaluate themselves or to compare themselves with others, can do one another much violence, when it brings them some advantage, without conversely ever giving offence. In a word, every man, looking upon his fellowmen hardly differently from the way he looks upon animals of another species, can snatch the prey of the weaker or yield his own to the stronger, without envisaging these thefts as anything but natural events, without the least feeling of insolence or spite, and without any other passion but the joy of success or the sorrow of failure.

(P) It is an extremely remarkable thing that after the many years that Europeans have spent tormenting themselves to convert the savages of the various countries of the world to their way of life, they have not been able yet to win a single one, not even with the blessing of Christianity, for our missionaries sometimes make Christians of savages, but never civilized men. Nothing can overcome the invincible repugnance they have against adopting our morals and living in our style. If these savages are as unhappy as it is claimed, by what inconceivable depravity of judgement do they refuse steadfastly to civilize themselves in imitation of us and to live happily among us, whereas one reads in a thousand places that Frenchmen and other Europeans have voluntarily found refuge among these peoples, spent their whole lives there without being able to leave such a strange way of life, and we see sensible missionaries tenderly lamenting calm and innocent days spent among those much despised peoples? If one suggests that savages have not enlightenment enough to judge their own condition or ours, I shall reply that the judgement of happiness is less an affair of reason than of feeling. Besides, this point can be turned against us with even more force, for there is a greater distance between our ideas and the capacities of mind needed for us to understand the savages' taste for their way of life than between the ideas of savages and the capacities of mind needed for them to understand ours. In fact, after a few observations it is easy for them to see that all our labours are directed towards two objectives only: namely, commodities of life for oneself and consideration from others. But how are we to imagine the kind of pleasure a savage takes in spending his life alone in the depths of the woods, or fishing, or blowing into a bad flute, not knowing how to produce a single note from it, or troubling to learn how to do so?

On several occasions savages have been brought to Paris or London or other cities; we have hastened to show off to them our luxury, our riches, and all our most useful and curious arts; all of which has never excited in them anything but stupid admiration, without the least emotion of covetousness. I remember among others the story of a North American chief who was brought to the Court in England some thirty years ago. A thousand things were put before his eyes in the search for a present that would please him, but nothing could be found which he appeared to like. Our weapons seemed heavy and incommodious to him; our shoes hurt his feet, our clothes constrained him; he rejected everything. Finally, it was noticed that having taken a woollen blanket, he seemed to enjoy wrapping it round his shoulders. 'You would agree at least', someone promptly said to him, 'that this article is useful?' 'Yes', he replied, 'it seems to me almost as good as an animal skin.' He would not have said even that if he had worn them both under the rain.

Perhaps, someone will say to me, it is habit which, by attaching everyone to his own way of life, prevents the savage from sensing what is good in ours. On this argument, it must seem at least very extraordinary that habit has more power to keep savages in their taste for their misery than to keep Europeans in the enjoyment of their felicity. But to answer this last objection with a reply to which there can be no word of rejoinder – without mentioning all the young savages we have endeavoured fruitlessly to civilize, without speaking of the Greenlanders and inhabitants of Iceland they attempted to educate and feed in Denmark, and who all died of sorrow and despair, either from wasting away or drowning in the sea when they tried to return to their homes by swimming.[45] I shall be content to quote a single well-attested example, which I submit to the scrutiny of admirers of European civilization:

'All the efforts of the Dutch missionaries at the Cape of Good Hope have never been able to convert a single Hottentot. Van der Stel, Governor of the Cape, having taken one in infancy, had him brought up in the principles of the Christian religion and the practice of the customs of Europe. He was finely dressed, and taught several languages, and his progress matched the care taken of his upbringing. The Governor, pinning high hopes on his intelligence, sent him to the Indies with a commissioner-general who employed him usefully in the business of the Company. He returned to the Cape on the death of the commissioner. A few days after his return, on a visit to some of his Hottentot kinsfolk, he decided to strip off his European finery in order to clothe himself in a sheepskin. He returned to the fort in this new garb, carrying a parcel which contained his former clothes, and presenting them to the Governor, he made the following speech: "Have the goodness, Sir, to observe that I renounce this apparel for ever. I also renounce for the rest of my life the Christian religion. My resolution is to live and die in the religion, the customs and usages of my ancestors. The one favour I ask of you is to allow me to keep the necklace and the cutlass I am wearing. I shall keep them for the love of you." Immediately, without waiting for Van der Stel's reply, he took to his heels to escape and was never seen again at the Cape.'*

(Q) One might object that amidst a disorder of this kind men, instead of stubbornly murdering each other, would have scattered if there had been no boundary to halt their dispersal. But first of all, these boundaries would at least have been those of the world; and if one thinks of the excessive population which results from the state of nature, one will conclude that the earth in that state would soon be covered with men, forced to remain together. Besides, they would have scattered if the evil had been swift, and had it been a change happening from one day to the next; but they were born under the yoke; they were in the habit of bearing it when they came to feel its weight, and they were content to wait for the opportunity to shake it off. In the end, already accustomed to a thousand advantages which forced them to remain together, dispersal was no longer as easy as it was

* *Histoire générale des voyages*, vol. V, p. 175.

in the earliest times when, no one having any need of anyone but himself, everyone made his decisions without waiting for the agreement of another.

(R) Field Marshal de V———* related that during one of his campaigns, the excessive cheating of a supply-contractor having caused suffering and protests in the army, he took the man to task and threatened to have him hanged. 'The threat does not trouble me,' the knave replied boldly, 'and I am relieved to tell you that they do not hang a man with a hundred thousand crowns at his disposal.' 'I do not know how it happened,' the Marshal naïvely commented, 'but in fact the man was not hanged, even though he deserved it a hundred times.'

(S) Distributive justice would even be opposed to that rigorous equality of the state of nature, even if it were practicable in civil society, and as all members of the state owe it services proportionate to their talents and their strength, the citizens in turn ought to be honoured and favoured in proportion to their services. It is in this sense that we should understand a passage in Isocrates where he praises the first Athenians for having known how to distinguish the more advantageous of the two sorts of equality, one of which consists of giving the same advantages to all citizens indifferently and the other of distributing them according to the merit of each citizen. These able politicians, adds the orator, banishing that unjust equality which recognizes no distinction between bad and good people, stood steadfastly by that which rewards and punishes everyone according to his merit. But in the first place there has never existed a society, at whatever stage of corruption it might have reached, in which no difference is recognized between bad and good people, and in matters of morals, where the law cannot lay down precise enough lines to serve as a rule for the magistrate, the law very wisely, to avoid leaving the fortune or rank of citizens to his discretion, forbids him to judge persons and leaves him to judge only actions. Only morals as pure as those of the ancient Romans can endure censors, and among us such tribunals would soon have overthrown everything. It is for public

---

* Maréchal-Duc de Villars.

esteem to establish the difference between bad and good men. The magistrate is the judge only of what is strictly law; the people are the true judge of morals – an upright and indeed an enlightened judge on this point, sometimes abused but never corrupted. The ranking of citizens ought therefore to be regulated, not according to their personal merit, which would leave the magistrate with the means of making an almost arbitrary application of the law, but according to the real services they render to the State, which are susceptible of a more exact measurement.

ABBREVIATIONS USED IN EDITOR'S INTRODUCTION AND NOTES

Annales	*Annales de la Société Jean-Jacques Rousseau*, Geneva, 1905– .
BVN	Bibliothèque de la Ville de Neuchâtel, Switzerland.
CC	*Correspondance complète de J.-J. Rousseau*, ed. R. A. Leigh, Geneva, Banbury and Oxford, 1965– .
Essai	J.-J. Rousseau, *Essai sur l'origine des langues*, ed. C. Porset, Bordeaux and Paris, 1970.
Havens	G. R. Havens, *Voltaire's Marginalia on the Pages of Rousseau*, Columbus, Ohio, 1933.
J.-J.	M. Cranston, *Jean-Jacques: the Early Life and Work of Jean-Jacques Rousseau, 1712–1754*, London and New York, 1983.
OC	*Œuvres complètes de J.-J. Rousseau*, ed. for the Bibliothèque de la Pléiade by B. Gagnebin *et al.*, Paris, 1959– .
OPB	*Œuvres philosophiques de Buffon*, ed. J. Piveteau, Paris, 1954.
PMLA	Proceedings of the Modern Language Association.
Reappraisals	*Reappraisals of Rousseau*, ed. S. Harvey *et al.*, Manchester, 1980.
RHLF	*Revue d'histoire littéraire de la France.*
SC	J.-J. Rousseau, *The Social Contract*, trans. M. Cranston, Harmondsworth and Baltimore, 1968.
SVEC	*Studies on Voltaire and the Eighteenth Century*, ed. T. Besterman and H. Mason, Geneva and Oxford, 1960– .
Wokler I	'Perfectible Apes in a Decadent Culture – Rousseau's Anthropology Revisited', in *Daedalus*, vol. 107, no. 3, 1978, pp. 107–34.
Wokler II	R. Wokler, 'The *Discours sur l'inégalité* and its sources', in *SVEC* (forthcoming).

EDITOR'S NOTES

THE DISCOURSE

1. Rousseau refers to the Treaty of Turin which had settled all residual differences between the Republic of Geneva and the Kingdom of Sardinia, her oldest enemy; and guaranteed her frontiers (see *J.-J.*, pp. 326–7).

2. Rousseau refers here to the rebellion of the liberal citizens against the conservative patrician regime which carried Geneva to the brink of Civil War in 1737 (see *J.-J.*, p. 125).

3. Rousseau had never any patience with feminism, although he had been employed, as a young man, as research assistant to Mme Dupin, an early champion of women's liberation. In *Émile* (Book V, written in 1759) he explains at length why the upbringing of a girl (Sophie) must be different from that of a boy (Émile). 'The more women want to resemble men, the less they will govern them; and then men really will be the masters' (*OC*, IV, p. 701). See also R. Shackleton, 'Montesquieu, Dupin and the early writings of Rousseau', *Reappraisals*, pp. 234–49.

4. There is evidence to suggest that Rousseau originally designed a much longer essay than the *Discourse* as it finally appeared (see R. A. Leigh, 'Manuscrits disparus', *Annales*, XXXIV, pp. 62–76). Among other things, Rousseau drafted a section on the origin of religion, and then deleted it, perhaps because he was going through a period of acute re-appraisal of his own feelings about religion (see *J.-J.*, pp. 310–23, and Starobinski, *OC*, III, p. 1378). This discarded draft (*OC*, III, pp. 224–5) contains some anti-clerical polemics characteristic of the *cercle holbachique*, but not at all characteristic of Rousseau, and may well have been one of the pieces suggested to him by Diderot. Wokler has identified several other fragments of the *Discourse* (see Wokler, II).

5. Jean-Jacques Burlamaqui (1694–1748), Genevan jurist and celebrated exponent of the natural law theory. Rousseau's reference is to *Principes du droit naturel*, Geneva, 1747, chap. I, § 2. On Rousseau's debts to the natural law theorists see R. Derathé, *Rousseau et la science politique de son temps*, Paris, 1950.

6. These words may explain why Rousseau places so little emphasis on the second part of the question posed by the Dijon Academy for competitors to answer: 'What is the origin of inequality among men and *is it authorized by natural law*?' Rousseau chooses instead to add to the question of the origin of inequality the question of the *foundations* of inequality. Both Hobbes and

Locke assign to natural man a rationality capable of discerning natural law and enabling men to contract together to quit the state of nature. Rousseau's denial of natural man's rationality precludes the kind of social contract which both Hobbes and Locke describe, and prepares the way for the formulation of a very different kind of contract.

7. According to Kant, in a world which needs rules of natural law but cannot derive that law from nature, 'practical reason' provides an alternative source. See E. Cassirer, *The Problem of J.-J. Rousseau*, (trans. P. Gay) New York, 1954.

8. The 'facts' Rousseau proposes to set aside are perhaps those of Holy Scripture; by calling them 'facts' he placates the Christian establishment, and claims for his own method of hypothesis and rational reconstruction the status of science. See C. Lévi-Strauss, 'J.-J. Rousseau, fondateur des sciences de l'homme', in *J.-J. Rousseau*, Neuchâtel, 1962, p. 240; *Tristes tropiques*, Paris, 1955, p. 423, and *Le Totémisme aujourd'hui*, Paris, 1962, pp. 142–6. See also J. Derrida, *De la grammatologie*, Paris, 1967, pp. 149–202; Wokler, I, pp. 107–17; R. Meek, *Social Science and the Ignoble Savage*, Cambridge, 1976; M. Duchet, *Anthropologie et histoire au siècle des lumières*, Paris, 1971, R. Wokler, 'Le "Discours sur les sciences et les arts" and its offspring', *Reappraisals*, pp. 250–78.

PART ONE

1. The idea of primitive man had already by Rousseau's time a long history. See A. O. Lovejoy and George Boas, *A Documentary History of Primitivism in Antiquity*, Baltimore, 1935; R. Bernheimer, *Wild Man in the Middle Ages*, Cambridge, Mass., 1952; A. Pagden, *The Fall of Natural Man*, Cambridge, 1983.

2. Voltaire underlined 'kills them indiscriminately' in his copy and added: 'obscure and ill-placed'. *Voltaire's Marginalia on the Pages of Rousseau*, ed. G. R. Havens, Ohio, 1933, contains numerous such sharp comments on the *Discourse on Inequality* which will be translated and reproduced in these notes. H. Gouhier (*Rousseau et Voltaire*, Paris, 1983, pp. 7–194) provides a detailed study of the relationship between the two philosophers. See also R. Pomeau, 'Voltaire, Rousseau: deux débats', *Annales*, XXXIX, 1972–7.

3. What Hobbes says is that man is naturally aggressive, not naturally intrepid; and indeed Hobbes suggests that this aggressiveness springs from fear as much as from vainglorious egoism (see *De Cive*, I, 4 and 12; *Leviathan*, I, 13). It is doubtful whether Rousseau had more than a scanty knowledge of Hobbes's work, impressed as he was by what he did know. He may have acquired some

of his ideas about Hobbes from Diderot, who knew English as well as Latin. See Wokler, *SVEC*, 1975, CXXXII, pp. 55–112.

4. Richard Cumberland (1631–1718), a seventeenth-century critic of Hobbes and author of *De Legibus naturae*, London, 1670, which Rousseau had read in J. Barbeyrac's translation, *Traité philosophique des loix naturelles*, Amsterdam, 1744. The 'illustrious philosopher' with whom Cumberland agrees is Montesquieu (*L'Esprit des lois*, I, ii).

5. Samuel Pufendorf (1632–94), author of *De Jure naturale*, Lund, 1672, translated as *Le Droit de la nature et des gens*, by J. Barbeyrac, Amsterdam, 1718. Rousseau speaks in the *Confessions* of having a book by Pufendorf in the bedroom he occupied at Annecy at the age of seventeen (*OC*, I, p. 110).

6. *Les Voyages de François Coréal aux Indes occidentales*, Paris, 2 vols, 1722. See also G. Pire, 'J.-J. Rousseau et les relations de voyages', *RHLF*, LVI, 1956, pp. 355–78.

7. Buffon drew much the same contrast between healthy animals and unhealthy men. See *Histoire naturelle*, 1753, VII, pp. 66–8. See also Hester Hastings, *Man and Beast in French Thought of the Eighteenth Century*, Oxford, 1936.

8. Coréal, op. cit., vol. I, p. 85.

9. Jean Laët (1593–1649), Flemish naturalist, author of *L'Histoire du nouveau monde*, Leyden, 1650, on p. 143 of which the tlaquatzin is described.

10. Rousseau derived his knowledge of the Hottentots from Peter Kolben, whose *Description du Cap de Bonne Espérance*, Amsterdam, 1741, was reprinted in vol. V of the *Histoire générale des voyages*, Paris, 1748.

11. For Rousseau's knowledge of the American savages, see J. Morel, 'Recherches sur les sources du *Discours de l'inégalité*', *Annales*, vol. V, 1909, pp. 119–98, and G. Chinard, *L'Amérique: le rêve exotique dans la littérature française aux XVIIe et XVIIIe siècles*, Paris, 1934.

12. 'Pretty bad metaphysics', wrote Voltaire in the margin of his copy (Havens, p. 6). However, Buffon says something very similar to Rousseau about the difference between man, with his 'spiritual principle', and animals, with their 'material internal sense' (*Histoire naturelle*, 1752, vol. IV, pp. 167–8).

13. The word Rousseau uses is '*perfectibilité*', at that time a neologism. It did not appear in the Fourth Edition (1740) of the *Dictionnaire* of the French Academy, but does appear in the Fifth Edition (1798). Turgot is reported to have used the word in conversation from 1750 onwards (*OC*, III, p. 1317). See also R. Wokler, 'Rousseau's Perfectibilian Liberalism', in A. Ryan, ed., *The Idea of Freedom*, Oxford, 1979, pp. 233–52.

14. F. Coréal, op. cit., vol. I, pp. 260–61 records their practice.

15. Here Rousseau develops an idea drawn from Montesquieu. See R. Shackleton, 'The evolution of Montesquieu's theory of climate', in *Revue internationale de philosophie*, IX, 1955, pp. 317–29.

16. Voltaire disagreed. 'No, they make Gods of their benefactors' (Havens, p. 8).

17. 'Rousseau is going to postulate here a series of hypotheses, less to formulate a coherent theory of the origin of language than to show the difficulties which the problem raises ... Against the philosophers who with Aristotle define man by sociability and language, Rousseau undertakes to prove that sociability and language are not attributes belonging to the essence of man, but acquisitions gained in the course of a long history.' Starobinski (*OC*, III, pp. 1322–3).

18. Rousseau had made the acquaintance of Condillac when, at the age of twenty-eight, he had found employment as tutor to the two sons of M. de Mably, Provost of the Lyonnais. Condillac was a younger brother of Mably and lived in the same house at the time. Later in Paris, Rousseau and Condillac saw each other often, and it was Rousseau who found a publisher for Condillac's celebrated *Essai* (see *J.-J.*, pp. 142 and 217–19).

Rousseau's theory of language was based on that of Condillac, but he did not accept the view of Condillac that thought was independent of speech, and that words stood for ideas in the mind. Rousseau has a good deal more to say about language in his unfinished, posthumously published *Essai sur les origines des langues*. See J. Derrida, 'La linguistique de Rousseau', *Revue internationale de philosophie*, LXXXII, 1967, pp. 448–52; A. Verri, 'On the Porset edition of Rousseau's *Essai*', *SVEC*, CLV, 1976, pp. 2167–71, and R. Wokler, 'L'*Essai* en tant que fragment du *Discours*', in M. Launay, ed., *Rousseau et Voltaire en 1978*, Geneva, 1981, pp. 145–69. A translation by J. H. Moran of Rousseau's *Essay on the Origin of Languages* was published in New York in 1966.

19. Voltaire's comment: 'Ridiculous supposition' (Havens, p. 9).

20. Voltaire's comment: 'They all were at least called AB because they resemble A' (Havens, p. 9).

21. Voltaire's comment: 'Pitiful!' (Havens, p. 9).

22. Voltaire's comment: 'Because there is an instinct and an aptitude in a man that there is not in a monkey (Havens, p. 10).'

23. Rousseau's reference is presumably to *De Cive*, chap. X, §1. But see note 3 above.

24. Voltaire's comment: 'The savage is wicked only as a wolf is hungry' (Havens, p. 10).

25. Bernard (de) Mandeville (1670–1733), Anglo-Dutch philosopher, whose *The Fable of the Bees, or Private Vices Public Benefits* first appeared in London in 1723. The French translation *La Fable des abeilles* was published in Amsterdam in 1740.

26. Rousseau is thinking of La Rochefoucauld's epigram: 'Pity is often a feeling of our own misfortune in the misfortune of another; we give help to others to oblige them to help us in similar circumstances.'

27. Voltaire's comment: 'What an idea! Must we then have reasoning in order to will our own wellbeing?' (Havens, p. 10).

28. In the *Confessions* (*OC*, I, p. 389) Rousseau says in a footnote that he took from Diderot this remark about the philosopher putting his hands over his ears to harden his heart against the cries of a man being murdered. But Rousseau himself had already published something similar in the preface to *Narcisse*: 'The taste for philosophy slackens all bounds of sympathy and goodwill which join men to society' (*OC*, II, p. 967). On Diderot's influence over Rousseau, and Rousseau's over Diderot, see G. Chinard's edition of Diderot's *Supplément au voyage de Bougainville*, Paris, 1935; J. Fabre, 'Deux frères ennemis' and G. R. Havens, 'Diderot, Rousseau and the *Discours sur l'inégalité*', both in *Diderot Studies*, III, Geneva, 1961, pp. 155–213 and pp. 219–62; A. Adam, 'Rousseau et Diderot', in *Revue des sciences humaines*, vol. 53, pp. 21–34, and Starobinski (*OC*, III, pp. 1332–4). J. Morel, in 'Recherches sur les sources du *Discours de l'inégalité*' (*Annales*, V, p. 124), notes that Rousseau moves from accusing Diderot of giving bad advice to accusing him of inserting whole bits of text. See also R. Wokler, *SVEC*, CXXXII, 1975, pp. 55–112.

29. Voltaire's comment: 'Fool that you are, don't you know that the North American Indians exterminated themselves in wars?' (Havens, p. 11).

30. Voltaire's comment: 'Ought to obey? Why?' (Havens, p. 12). Against Rousseau's belief in the natural inequality of women, Voltaire always asserted their equality with men: 'Women are capable of doing everything we do: the only difference between them and us is that they are nicer (*plus aimables*)', Voltaire, *Correspondance*, ed. Besterman, V, p. 279.

31. Voltaire's comment: 'How do you know? Have you ever seen savages making love?' (Havens, p. 13).

32. Voltaire's comment: 'More males are actually born, but at the end of twenty years the number of females is greater' (Havens, p. 13).

33. Voltaire's comment: 'It is to conclude with a piece of very bad fiction' (Havens, p. 14).

34. Voltaire's comment: 'Beauty excites love and intelligence produces the arts' (Havens, p. 14).

35. Voltaire's comment: 'What, can you not see that mutual needs have done it all?' (Havens, p. 15).

PART TWO

1. Voltaire's comment: 'What! He who has planted, sown, and enclosed some land has no right to the fruit of his efforts! Is this unjust man, this thief to be the benefactor of the human race? Behold the philosophy of a beggar who would like the rich to be robbed by the poor!' (Havens, p. 15).

2. See Richard Schlatter, *Private Property: the History of an Idea*, London, 1951. For Locke's theory of a natural right to property, see W. von Leyden, *Hobbes and Locke*, London, 1982.

It is worth noting that Rousseau, in his article on *'l'Économie politique'* written for Diderot's *Encyclopaedia* at about the same time as the *Discourse on Inequality*, makes at least two wholly Lockean assertions about property: 'It is certain that the right to property is the most sacred of all the rights of citizens and more important in certain respects than liberty itself' (*OC*, III, p. 263); 'We must remember here that the basis of the social contract is property, and its first stipulation is that everyone be assured of the peaceful enjoyment of what belongs to him' (*OC*, III, pp. 269–70). See also Derathé's introduction to the 'Économie politique' (*OC*, III, pp. lxxii–lxxxi), C. W. Hendel, *Jean-Jacques Rousseau Moralist*, New York, 1934, I, p. 98, and *J.-J.*, pp. 247–8.

3. On the significance of 'obstacles' in Rousseau's thought, see J. Starobinski, *J.-J. Rousseau: la transparence et l'obstacle*, Paris, 1958.

4. Voltaire's comment: 'Ridiculous' (Havens, p. 16).

5. See Rousseau's remarks on incest in the *Essai*, p. 125.

6. Voltaire's comment: 'A passion which receives sacrifices' (Havens, p. 16).

7. On Rousseau's ideas about man's original innocence, see J. S. Spink, *Rousseau et Genève*, Paris, 1934; J. F. Thomas, *Le Pélagianisme de J.-J. Rousseau*, Paris, 1956; P. M. Masson, *La Formation réligieuse de Rousseau*, Paris, three vols., 1916.

8. Rousseau, who read Locke only in translation, refers to Pierre Coste's edition of *Essai philosophique concernant l'entendement humain*, Amsterdam, 1723, Book IV, iii, §18. However, Rousseau makes a curious mistake in doing so, for he uses the word *'injure'* whereas Coste translates Locke's word 'injustice' correctly as *'injustice'*: i.e. *'il ne sauroit y avoir de l'injustice où il n'y a point de propriété'*.

9. Voltaire's comment: 'What a chimera is this golden mean!' (Havens, p. 17).

10. Voltaire's comment: 'The Mexicans and Peruvians who were subjugated by the Spanish savages were very civilized. Mexico City was as beautiful as Amsterdam' (Havens, pp. 17–18).

11. Voltaire's comment: 'False' (Havens, p. 18).

12. Voltaire's comment: 'Iron is produced in great quantities in the Pyrenees' (Havens, p. 19).

13. Rousseau's thinking reappears in the modern theory of a neolithic revolution introducing the culture of the soil and breeding of animals before the appearance of the palaeometalic age (see V. Gordon Childe, *The Prehistory of European Society*, London, 1958).

14. 'Rousseau's ideal is independent work, of the artisan type. All division of labour, all subordination is hateful to him' (Starobinski, *OC*, III, p. 1347).

15. In his *Lettre à Christophe de Beaumont*, Rousseau writes: 'As soon as I was in a state to observe men, I watched them all and I heard them speak; then, seeing that their actions in no way resembled their words, I sought the reason for this disjunction, and I found that being and appearing were two things as different from each other as were acting and speaking, and that this second difference was the cause of the other, and had itself a cause it remained for one to seek.

'I found it in our social order which, being at every point opposed to nature which nothing destroyed, tyrannized it ceaselessly and made it ceaselessly demand its rights. I followed this contradiction in its consequences, and I saw that it alone explained all men's vices and all the evils of society. From this I concluded that it was not necessary to suppose man wicked by nature, when one could trace the origin and the progress of his wickedness' (*Collection complète des œuvres de J.-J. Rousseau*, Brussels, 1804, vol. XI, pp. 88–9).

16. Already in his reply to King Stanislas's criticisms of his first *Discourse*, Rousseau had written: 'The first source of evil is inequality; from inequality came riches ... and from riches arose luxury and idleness; from luxury arose the fine arts and from idleness the sciences' (*OC*, III, p. 49).

17. It is important to distinguish the 'fraudulent' social contract described in this *Discourse* from the 'authentic' social contract envisaged in Rousseau's book entitled *Du contrat social* (1762). In that later work, Rousseau examines the kind of covenant which would enable man at the same time to enter civil society and remain free: it is essentially a contract by which each alienates his natural rights in return for civil rights and submits only to a sovereign body of which he is himself a member (*SC*, pp. 59–62). The *Discourse* describes what did happen, or rather must have happened: the *Social Contract* describes what would need to happen to produce a certain result (the fusion of liberty and law).

18. It is instructive to compare Rousseau's views on the origins of civil society with those of Diderot. (See J. Proust, *Diderot et l'Encyclopédie*, Paris, 1967) and Hobbes (*Leviathan*, XIII). For Diderot society is natural; for Hobbes the social contract is a rational response to a state of war. For Rousseau (in this *Discourse*) it is a trick perpetrated by the corrupt rich on the unsuspecting but equally corrupt multitude.

19. Starobinski points out that the development of human society is seen by Rousseau as passing through a series of revolutions: (1) Man, originally idle, discovers the utility of work and of collaborating with other men in such activities as hunting. (2) Man learns to build himself a dwelling and this transforms a solitary being, who had neither settled mate nor known offspring, into a family-man and a patriarch. This period Rousseau considers the 'golden age' of the human race. (3) Men, by a 'fatal accident', discover the division of labour, which leads them to pass from a subsistence economy to a productive economy. Agriculture and metallurgy have the ruinous consequence of enabling men to produce more than they need for immediate consumption. Then they quarrel about what is left over. (4) Agricultural man can protect the produce of his labour only by enclosing the land he has planted. So he proclaims himself proprietor. But in the absence of a system of law, he has possession without rightful property, and here Rousseau joins Hobbes in visualizing a 'horrible state of war' of each against all. (5) In order to escape this state of war, men accept a 'social contract' devised by the rich to ensure peace for everybody and rightful ownership for those in possession, a 'contract' which the poor, desiring peace, are swindled into accepting. This introduces, with civil society, the institution and enforcement of law (*OC*, III, pp. lxii–lxv).

20. A copy of the *Discourse* which Rousseau presented to Richard Davenport in 1767 contains an interesting correction in his hand: he alters the reference to 'great cosmopolitan souls breaking through imaginary barriers and following the example of the Sovereign Being' to 'great cosmopolitan souls worthy to break through the imaginary barriers that separate peoples and of embracing the whole human race, following the example of the Supreme Being who created it'. See C. A. Rochedieu, 'Notes marginales', *Annales*, XXV, pp. 267–72.

21. Rousseau seems to have in mind La Fontaine's fable 'The old man and the ass' (Book VI of the *Fables*, no. 8).

22. Pliny, '*Elogium of Trajan*', LV. §7.

23. Rousseau owes this quotation to Algernon Sidney (1622–83) whose *Discourse Concerning Government*, London, 1698, he was reading in a French translation, *Discours sur le gouvernement*, The Hague, 3 vols, 1702.

24. See Pufendorf, *Le Droit de la nature et des gens*, VII, chap. iii, §1.

EDITOR'S NOTES *pp. 127–39*

25. Rousseau cites Barbeyrac from Pufendorf, op. cit., VII, chap. viii, §6.

26. Voltaire's comment: 'very fine' (Havens, pp. 19–20).

27. Leigh has published (*Annales*, XXXIV, 1956–8, pp. 71–7) some excerpts from an earlier draft of the *Discourse*, in which Rousseau enlarges on this theme.

28. Voltaire's comment: 'Ape of Diogenes, how you condemn yourself!' (Havens, p. 21).

29. Voltaire's comment: 'How you exaggerate everything! How you put it all in a false light!' (Havens, p. 21).

30. '*Pectore si fratris gladium juguloque parentis condere me jubeas, gravidaeque in viscera partu conjugis, invitâ peragam tamen omnia dextra.*' Rousseau takes this quotation from Algernon Sidney's *Discourses Concerning Government*, London, 1698, p. 147, where Lucan's '*plenaeque*' is rendered as '*gravidaeque*'.

31. Voltaire's comment: 'If royal power *did* hold everyone under its sway and suppress all factions, you would be paying the highest tribute to the Kings against whom you declaim' (Havens, p. 22).

32. '*Cui ex honesto nulla est spes*' is a modified quotation from Tacitus that Rousseau probably read in Sidney's *Discours sur le gouvernement*, The Hague, 1702, § XIX.

33. 'In essence ... Rousseau's description of the original savage overturned the principal barriers that Buffon had constructed between man and beast' (Wokler, I).

'One could say that Rousseau, in order to paint natural man, animalizes ... man as he is described by Buffon' (Starobinski, *J.-J. Rousseau: la transparence et l'obstacle*, revised edition, Paris, 1971, p. 387).

For Rousseau's importance to modern sociobiology see R. Masters, 'Jean-Jacques is alive and well', in *Daedelus*, vol. 107, no. 3, 1978, pp. 93–105.

34. 'Rousseau is not demanding the equalization and the levelling of conditions; he wishes only that civil inequality should be proportionate to the natural inequality of talents' (Starobinski, *OC*, III, p. lxix).

NOTES ON ROUSSEAU'S NOTES

1. Rousseau is referring here to Buffon. It is said that when Rousseau visited Buffon's house in Montbard in 1770 he 'threw himself on his knees and kissed the threshold of the door' (see M. J. Herault de Séchelles, *Œuvres littéraires*, Paris, 1907, p. 13). The two philosophers had first met in 1742, when Rousseau was working as a research assistant to Mme Dupin, and remained on very

friendly terms, although Buffon was revolted by Rousseau's posthumous *Confessions*: 'I ceased to esteem him ... I began to think ill of him' (op. cit., p. 24). On the complex question of Rousseau's intellectual debts to Buffon, and his disagreements with Buffon, see Wokler, I. O. Fellows, 'Buffon and Rousseau', PMLA, LXXV, 1960; B. Glass et al., eds, *Forerunners of Darwin*, Baltimore, 1968; E. Guyénot, *Les Sciences de la vie au XVIIe et XVIIIe siècles*, Paris, 1941; Mornet, *Les sciences de la nature en France, au XVIIIe siècle*, Paris, 1911; J. Starobinski, 'Rousseau et Buffon', in *J.-J. Rousseau: la transparence et l'obstacle*, Paris, 1971.

2. Rousseau refers to Buffon's *Histoire naturelle, générale et particulière*, in -- 12°, Paris, 1752. Buffon was not an evolutionist: 'It is certain, through revelation, that all the animals participated equally in the grace of Creation, and that the first of each species and of every species emerged fully formed from the hands of the Creator, and one must believe that they were more or less the same then as they are today represented by their descendants' (*OPB*, p. 355).

3. See Condillac's *Essai sur l'origine des connaissances humaines*, 1746, l, iv, §23. Condillac owed the anecdote to Bernard Connor's *Evangelium medicum*, London, 1697, pp. 133–4.

4. See J. A. L. Single and M. Zingg, *Wolf-children and Feral Man*, New York, 1942.

5. Buffon's *Histoire naturelle* finally ran to forty-four volumes (Paris, 1749–1804). Rousseau consulted while writing the present *Discours* the first four volumes, which were published in 12° edition in 1752–3.

6. See also R. Masters, *The Political Philosophy of Rousseau*, Princeton, 1968, pp. 122–5.

7. Starobinski suggests that Rousseau made this experiment at Les Charmettes, where he lived between 1735 and 1737 (*OC*, III, p. 1362).

8. Rousseau may have read in Buffon's *Histoire naturelle*, vol. VIII, p. 89, of the 1753 in 12° Paris edition that 'man could live like an ox on vegetables', but Buffon subsequently rejected Rousseau's conclusion that man was naturally vegetarian. In vol. XIV, p. 44, of the 1764 in 12° Paris edition of his *Histoire naturelle*, Buffon wrote: 'abstinence from all flesh, far from conforming to Nature, could only destroy man'.

9. Rousseau's source is *Voyages de François Coréal aux Indes occidentales*, 2 vols, Paris, I, p. 40.

10. Peter Kolben, Dutch traveller and author of *Description du Cap de Bonne-Espérance*, Amsterdam, 1742. The source Rousseau cites is *Histoire générale des voyages*, ed. A. F. Prévost, Paris, 20 vols, 1746–91, in which Kolben's work was reproduced with a commentary.

11. Rousseau seems to have misunderstood Kolben, who says that the Hottentots swim with their neck (*col*) not their body (*corps*) upright. Rousseau's manuscripts conserved at Neuchâtel contain several passages copied from Prévost's edition of Kolben on the subject of Hottentots which are not used in the present text. (See BVN. Ms. R. 18).

12. Le Père du Tertre, *Histoire générale des Antilles*, Paris, 1667–71, vol. VII, i, §5: 'De l'exerciee des sauvages.'

13. Rousseau refers to Jacques Gautier d'Agoty (1710–85), author of *Observations sur l'histoire naturelle, la physique et la peinture*, 3 vols, Paris, 1752–8.

14. Voltaire's comment: 'False: I have had two carriage horses which lived thirty-five years' (Havens, p. 23).

15. Rousseau refers to Pierre-Louis Moreau de Maupertuis (1698–1759), author of *Essai de philosophie morale* (Paris, 1730), the second chapter of which is headed: 'That in everyday life the sum of bad things exceeds that of good things.'

16. Rousseau has no conception of an inequality of distribution of wealth generating economic growth and an increase of overall wealth. For a comparison of Rousseau's views and those of Adam Smith see L. Colletti, *From Rousseau to Lenin*, pp. 154–9 and I. Fetscher, 'Rousseau's conception of freedom' in *Nomos*, IV, 1962. Adam Smith did not challenge Rousseau's economics in the review of the *Second Discourse* he wrote for the *Edinburgh Review*, 1755–6. He wrote rather of Rousseau as a follower of Mandeville, but possessed by a marvellous literary style: 'It is by the help of this style, together with a little philosophical chemistry, that the principles and ideas of the profligate Mandeville seem in him to have all the purity and sublimity of the morals of Plato.' See W. P. D. Wightman and S. C. Bryce (eds), *Adam Smith: Essays on Philosophical Subjects*, Oxford, 1980, pp. 242–55.

17. Voltaire's comment: 'And still more of every savage, if it were possible' (Havens, p. 23)

18. Rousseau sent to the *Mercure de France* a letter (published in the issue of July, 1953, pp. 5–13) warning against the 'dangers' of using copper saucepans. More professional scientists argued that his fears were unfounded (see also *CC*, II, pp. 221–7).

19. Voltaire's comment: 'This sin has been found to be established in America; and in Jewish books that we are made to read, there is a people more barbarous than the sodomites' (Havens, p. 24).

20. Rousseau's own children were not 'exposed'; but in writing these lines, he must have been thinking of the five bastard offspring he had sent to the orphanage in Paris (see *J.-J.*, pp. 244–6).

21. Voltaire's comment: 'Unfortunate Jean-Jacques, whose debaucheries are well enough known, poor victim of the pox, do you not know it comes from savages?' (Havens, p. 24). There is no evidence that Rousseau had a venereal disease. He always denied it.

22. This whole paragraph was added to the text in a letter sent by Rousseau to his publisher Rey in February 1755 (*CC*, III, pp. 102–3). Rey printed Rousseau's word '*semblables*' (fellow-beings) as '*semblable*' (fellow-being).

23. A red arsenic 'used by goldsmiths to revive their gold' (see *Annales*, XIII, pp. 166–70).

24. Among the champions of luxury in the Enlightenment were Mandeville, Voltaire and Hume. See A. Morize, *L'apologie du luxe au XVIIIe siècle*, Paris, 1909; and E. Ross, 'The luxury controversy in France', *SVEC*, clv, 1976, pp. 1897–1912.

25. This paragraph was added to the text while it was in the press. See Rousseau's letter to M. M. Rey of 23 February 1755 (*CC*, III, p. 103).

26. Rousseau's approach to the evolution of species was one point of disagreement with Buffon, who repeatedly asserted the fixity of species. See A. O. Lovejoy, 'Buffon and the Problem of Species', in B. Glass, ed., *Forerunners of Darwin*, Baltimore, 1968. For an argument – to my mind, unconvincing – that Rousseau was as much a '*fixiste*' as Buffon see V. Goldschmidt, *Anthropologie et politique*, Paris, 1974.

27. The word 'orang-outang' comes from the Malay language, meaning 'man of the woods', and is used today to name only a kind of ape found in Indonesia. In the eighteenth century, however, all sorts of apes found in Africa and elsewhere were called 'orang-outangs' (see Wokler, I).

28. The most thoroughgoing champion of Rousseau's idea that the orang-outang was an animal of the human form was Lord Monboddo (see his *Of the Origin and Progress of Language*, second edition, Edinburgh, 1774). Dr Johnson said: 'Other people have strange notions, but they conceal them; if they have tails they hide them; but Monboddo is as jealous of his tail as a squirrel.' In France, some wag published a letter signed 'Rousseau, hitherto a civilized man and a Citizen of Geneva, but at present an orang-outang (*CC*, XII, p. 306). See A. O. Lovejoy, 'Monboddo and Rousseau', in *Essays in the History of Ideas*, Baltimore, 1948; R. Wokler, 'Tyson and Buffon on the orang-outang', in *SVEC*, CLV (1976), pp. 2301–19; 'The ape debates in Enlightenment anthropology', in *SVEC*, CXCLL, 1980, pp. 1164–75; and C. Frayling and R. Wokler, 'From orang-outang to vampire', in R. A. Leigh, ed., *Rousseau after Two Hundred Years*, Cambridge, 1981, pp. 109–29.

29. Andrew Battel (1565–1640?), an English traveller, explorer and adventurer captured by both the Indians of Brazil and the Portuguese in Angola, related his experiences to Samuel Purchas, an English editor and author.

30. The word used here is *nègres*, meaning black Africans. Buffon believed that all men were originally white (*Histoire naturelle*, III, p. 502) and that men's skins had become dark in Africa only as an effect of climate (op. cit., p. 483).

31. This French compilation contains material from different sources, including Battel.

32. Olfert Dapper (1630?–90), Dutch physician and geographer, was the author of numerous writings about the tropics. This quotation comes from his *Description de l'Afrique*, Amsterdam, 1686, pp. 365–6.

33. Jerome Merolla, born Sorrento, c. 1650, was a Jesuit missionary who published a narrative of his travels as *Breve relazione del viaggio nel regno del Congo*, Naples, 1692.

34. In fact the *fourth* volume (Paris, 1747, pp. 240–41) contains the passage Rousseau cites: the spelling there is '*boggo*' and '*mandril*'.

35. Samuel Purchas (1577–1626), author of *Purchas his Pilgrimage*, London, 4 vols, 1625, which included an account of Andrew Battel's voyages. See Pire, 'Rousseau et les relations de voyages', *RHLF*, 1956, pp. 355–78.

36. The word Rousseau uses is '*philosophesque*', a neologism of his own invention designed to refer in a pejorative way to the *philosophes* of his time. In a letter to his publisher Rey dated 6 March 1755, Rousseau said: 'I beg you to take care that the printer sets "*tourbe philosophesque*" as written and not as "*tourbe philosophique*"' (*CC*, III, p. 105).

37. Charles-Marie de la Condamine (1701–74), author of *Relation abrégée du voyage fait à l'intérieur de l'Amérique méridionale*, Paris, 1745, was an acquaintance of Rousseau in Paris.

38. Rousseau refers to Maupertuis, *Relation d'un voyage au fond de la Lapponie*, Paris, 1738.

39. Jean Chardin (1643–1713), author of *Voyage en Perse et aux Indes orientales*, Amsterdam, 1711. Montesquieu also owed a great deal to Chardin in writing his *Les Lettres persanes*, Paris, 1721.

40. Engelbrecht Kaempfer (1651–1716), author of *A History of Japan*, London, 1727.

41. Buffon defended Locke's theory of the family as a natural society against Rousseau's objections (see the seventh volume of his *Histoire naturelle*, published in 1758, reproduced in *OPB*, pp. 373–4).

Rousseau himself, in *The Social Contract*, which he published in 1762 (seven years after the publication of the *Second Discourse*) asserts: 'the oldest of all societies and the only natural one is that of the family' (*SC*, p. 50). It is hard to resist the conclusion that Rousseau changed his mind on this subject.

42. Voltaire's comment: 'An abomination, Jean-Jacques ... All this is abominable, and shows a very bad knowledge of nature' (Havens, p. 26).

43. Plato's *Republic*, vii. §522.

44. The words Rousseau uses, *'amour de soi'* and *'amour-propre'* were not generally given by the philosophers of eighteenth-century France the meaning Rousseau gives them here. Rousseau seems to have taken these terms from the literature of religion. Masson, in his edition of *La Profession de foi du Vicaire savoyard* (Fribourg and Paris, 1914), discusses a number of the sources on which Rousseau may have drawn. On the importance of this distinction for Rousseau's social philosophy, see R. Polin, *La Politique de la solitude*, Paris, 1974; B. Baczko, *Rousseau, solitude et communauté*, Paris and The Hague, 1974; and J. Charvet, *The Social Problem in the Philosophy of Rousseau*, London, 1964. On Pascal's understanding of *amour-propre* see N. Keohane, *Philosophy and The State in France*, New York, 1975, pp. 266–77.

45. Rousseau's source is Isaac de la Peyrère, *Relation du Groenland*, Amsterdam, 1715, pp. 150–56.

PENGUIN ONLINE

News, reviews and previews of forthcoming books

read about your favourite authors

•

investigate over 12,000 titles

•

browse our online magazine

•

enter one of our literary quizzes

•

win some fantastic prizes in our competitions

•

e-mail us with your comments and book reviews

•

instantly order any Penguin book

'To be recommended without reservation ... a rich and rewarding online experience' *Internet Magazine*

www.penguin.com

read more

PENGUIN CLASSICS

THE COLLECTED LETTERS OF MARY WOLLSTONECRAFT

Mary Wollstonecraft is one of the most distinctive letter writers of the eighteenth century: to read her letters today is to trace her thoughts on paper. In this unique single volume of her correspondence, we follow her from the girl of fourteen leaving home to become a lady's companion, to the woman of thirty-eight, facing death in childbirth. The letters reveal her desire to reconcile personal integrity and sexual longing; motherhood and intellectual life; reason and passion. Touching and engaging, they form a compelling autobiographical document of one of Britain's most radical thinkers and writers.

Janet Todd's introduction places the letters in their biographical context and discusses Wollstonecraft's relationships with her correspondents. This edition also includes notes and an index.

'A remarkable record of intimate conversation 200 years ago, allowing us to eavesdrop on the past' Lydall Gordon, *Independent on Sunday*

'An exemplary edition ... providing vividly detailed and accessible footnotes' Kate Chisholm, *Telegraph*

Edited with an introduction and notes by Janet Todd

www.penguin.com

PENGUIN CLASSICS

THE HISTORY OF MARY PRINCE

The History of Mary Prince (1831) was the first narrative of a black woman to be published in Britain. It describes Prince's sufferings as a slave in Bermuda, Turks Island and Antigua, and her eventual arrival in London with her brutal owner Mr Wood in 1828. Prince escaped from him and sought assistance from the Anti-Slavery Society, where she dictated her remarkable story to Susanna Strickland (later Moodie). A moving and graphic document, *The History* drew attention to the continuation of slavery in the Caribbean, despite an 1807 Act of Parliament officially ending the slave trade. It inspired two libel actions and ran into three editions in the year of its publication. This powerful rallying cry for emancipation remains an extraordinary testament to Prince's ill-treatment, suffering and survival.

In her introduction, Sara Salih sets the work in its context as a significant early example of Black Atlantic literature. This edition also includes further reading, a chronology, the brief *Narrative of Louis Asa-Asa*, notes and appendices providing further contexts for Prince's *History*.

Edited with an introduction and notes by Sara Salih

THE STORY OF PENGUIN CLASSICS

Before 1946 ... 'Classics' are mainly the domain of academics and students; readable editions for everyone else are almost unheard of. This all changes when a little-known classicist, E. V. Rieu, presents Penguin founder Allen Lane with the translation of Homer's *Odyssey* that he has been working on in his spare time.

1946 Penguin Classics debuts with *The Odyssey*, which promptly sells three million copies. Suddenly, classics are no longer for the privileged few.

1950s Rieu, now series editor, turns to professional writers for the best modern, readable translations, including Dorothy L. Sayers's *Inferno* and Robert Graves's unexpurgated *Twelve Caesars*.

1960s The Classics are given the distinctive black covers that have remained a constant throughout the life of the series. Rieu retires in 1964, hailing the Penguin Classics list as 'the greatest educative force of the twentieth century.'

1970s A new generation of translators swells the Penguin Classics ranks, introducing readers of English to classics of world literature from more than twenty languages. The list grows to encompass more history, philosophy, science, religion and politics.

1980s The Penguin American Library launches with titles such as *Uncle Tom's Cabin*, and joins forces with Penguin Classics to provide the most comprehensive library of world literature available from any paperback publisher.

1990s The launch of Penguin Audiobooks brings the classics to a listening audience for the first time, and in 1999 the worldwide launch of the Penguin Classics website extends their reach to the global online community.

The 21st Century Penguin Classics are completely redesigned for the first time in nearly twenty years. This world-famous series now consists of more than 1300 titles, making the widest range of the best books ever written available to millions – and constantly redefining what makes a 'classic'.

The Odyssey continues ...

The best books ever written

PENGUIN CLASSICS

SINCE 1946

Find out more at www.penguinclassics.com